Your Magickal Cat

Also by Gerina Dunwich

Your Magickal Cat

Feline Magick, Lore, and Worship

Gerina Dunwich

𝒌

Citadel Press
Kensington Publishing Corp.
www.kensingtonbooks.com

CITADEL PRESS books are published by

Kensington Publishing Corp.
850 Third Avenue
New York, NY 10022

All Kensington titles, imprints, and distributed lines are available at special quantity discounts for bulk purchases for sales promotions, premiums, fund raising, educational, or institutional use. Special book excerpts or customized printings can also be created to fit specific needs. For details, write or phone the office of the Kensington special sales manager: Kensington Publishing Corp., 850 Third Avenue, New York, NY 10022, attn: Special Sales Department, phone 1-800-221-2647.

Kensington and the K logo Reg. U.S. Pat. & TM Office
Citadel Press is a trademark of Kensington Publishing Corp.

First printing 2000

Printed in the United States of America

10 9 8 7 6 5 4 3

Library of Congress Cataloging-in-Publication Data

Dunwich, Gerina.
    Your magickal cat : feline magick, lore, and worship / Gerina
Dunwich.
        p.   cm.
    "A Citadel Press book."
    Includes bibliographical references and index.
    ISBN 0–8065–2094–9 (pbk.)
    1. Magic. 2. Cats—Miscellanea. I. Title.
BF1623.A55D86   1999
133′.2599752—dc21   99–31181
                                                              CIP

This book is dedicated with love to my mother,
to Al, and to all of my cat friends and familiars:
Naomi, Gypsy, Simba, Oona, Stormy, Rama, Serena,
Merlin, Ian, Onya, Isadora, Endora, Esmerelda, Delilah,
Salem, Aleister, and Gemini. Blessed be!

Contents

Preface

I have been a cat-lover for as long as I can remember, even when I was a child and terribly allergic to them. Luckily, I overcame the sneezing, itchy eyes, and runny nose symptoms of my cat allergy by the time I reached my teen years and have shared my life with felines ever since.

Dogs have an uncanny way of sensing that I am a cat person and not a dog person. Most of them usually growl at me as though they can tell that when I'm old and senile I will probably end up being one of those weird witchy women in a rocking chair with hundreds of cats running amuck throughout the house.

With all of that said, when my editor phoned and asked me if I would be interested in writing a book about cats—with a magickal slant, of course—I was understandably quite delighted! It was a project that I couldn't wait to begin working on, and one that turned out to be immensely enjoyable.

After doing research for *Your Magickal Cat* for a little over a year, the manuscript was completed in the fall of 1998 and ready to be submitted to my editor at Citadel Press.

I was returning home from the local post office after putting the manuscript in the mail, and although I was excited about the book being finished, I could not help but feel a bit melancholy. I had just moved back to California from upstate New York, where I had to leave behind my thirteen cat-familiars: Merlin, Salem, Isadora, Endora, Serena, Ian, Onya, Spooky-Spirit, Esmerelda,

Delilah, Beltania, Aleister, and Quicksilver (who, sadly, had been diagnosed with feline leukemia). They had been a part of my life when I first began working on the book, but now that the book was done and it was time to celebrate, they were three thousand miles away, living in the new homes I had found for them.

My feline friends regularly participated in the many Wiccan rituals and Sabbat bonfires that my coven and I held at my old Victorian house in the country, and I loved each one of them dearly. I thought about how much I missed them and I asked the goddess Bastet (whom I had developed a deep respect and love for while writing this book) to watch over them. I then gave thanks to her for providing me with inspiration and spiritual guidance throughout the entire project; and when I returned home, she had a precious little gift waiting for me.

In my backyard near the swimming pool was a ginger tabby with the most unusual golden-colored eyes. He came right up to me without the slightest bit of fear or hesitation, as though he had known me for a long time. He allowed me to pick him up, and when I did, he filled my ears with the loudest purring I had ever heard coming from a cat.

He appeared to be about five months old, which placed his birthday somewhere between late May and early June, so I named him Gemini after his probable astrological sign. He responded to that name immediately and seemed to understand everything I said to him. I knew from the start that he was not an ordinary cat, especially since he sat on the roof at night to guard my house. He is my new familiar, and whenever I gaze into his mysterious golden eyes, I am reminded of the sun-drenched desert sand of Bastet's homeland.

I still miss my country cats back in upstate New York and the wonderful magickal times I spent with them, but my Gemini has managed to bring new love, joy, and cat-magick into this witch's life. I truly believe that he is a gift from the ancient cat-goddess—perhaps her way of thanking me for writing this book.

Introduction

Cats are, in this author's opinion, the most magickal of all creatures.
Worshipped in early times as a sacred animal, accused in the
Middle Ages of being the demonic helper of sorcerers, and regarded in modern times as having curative and longevity-
promoting powers, the furry feline has certainly earned its place
in history, literature, divination, religion, and the magickal arts.

To many people around the world (both cat-lovers and cat-
haters alike), the cat symbolizes the psychic and the occult, the
demonic and the divine, and the bridge between the darkness
of evil and the light of all that is good. Its power to stimulate
the human imagination is limitless, and by its own nature the
cat, whether she be a goddess in jewels or an ordinary house cat,
is a creature of great charm and mystery. It is no wonder that Sir
Walter Scott once said, "Ah, cats are a mysterious kind of folk."

Since the dawn of time, cats have been loved, hated, revered,
and feared. They have played the role of both devil and god/dess,
and they have found their way into innumerable fairy tales,
superstitions, spells, and myths. Playing a key role in Pagan religion and ritual, the magickal and mysterious ways of the cat conjure into being a wondrous world of legend and lore.

There is perhaps no other animal on this planet that comes
close to casting its spell of enchantment upon us quite as effectively or frequently as does the cat. With its exotic eyes, spark-
emitting fur, hypnotic purring, and often curious behavior, it is

not surprising that the cat has long been linked to the realms of the supernatural and all things of an esoteric nature.

Most modern witches, like those of olden times, have a strong and natural bond with cats that stretches back to times of antiquity. Throughout history they have employed cats as familiars to help raise energy and work magick, guard their magick circles, grace their coven-steads, heal the sick, acquire spiritual guidance, and divine the future.

Witches and cats also have much in common: Both are cloaked in mystery, associated with the powers of night and the moon, feared and misunderstood by many, attuned to the cycles of Mother Nature, and empowered with psychic sensitivity. And during what is now known as the "Burning Times," witch-cats were put on trial and forced to suffer torture and execution right alongside their human counterparts.

Many practitioners of the occult arts have long believed that cats' bodies are filled with an unexplainable magnetic energy. This peculiar feline magnetism is said to be highly powerful and has the power to either strongly attract or repel. (This may offer an explanation as to why most people either absolutely love cats or else totally hate them, but seldom do they possess indifferent feelings when it comes to this animal.)

Old Celtic legend holds that cats are "druidic beasts" and their eyes are windows to a mystical otherworld. With that in mind, and with this book in hand, prepare to gaze through those windows and explore the mysterious, magickal, metaphysical world of the cat.

JADE-EYED GODDESS

Waxing full and waning
With the moon of silver gleam,
Her eyes of jade do beckon
Like a mystery, like a dream.

No tigress lean or lioness brave
Could ever take her place.
No panther swift and black as night
Could make her fall from grace.

On Gypsy feet she prowls the eve,
A huntress in the darkness lurking.
Endless tales her shadows weave
Of wondrous things and witches' workings.

Hail to she with eyes of jade,
A precious gift, divinely made.
And bless her with a life times nine
O purring little goddess mine.

—from *Priestess and Pentacle*
by Gerina Dunwich

The author and one of her many
feline familiars from upstate New
York. (Photo by Al B. Jackter)

Your Magickal Cat

1

The Feline Divine

She wears the same voluptuous slow smile
She wore when she was worshipped on the Nile.
—Walter Adolphe Roberts

Nowhere in the world, at any time during the history of the human race, were cats more exalted and highly respected than in ancient Egypt. For it was there in that mysterious land of pyramids and pharaohs that great temples were built in honor of the feline; cat-shaped magickal charms were worn for protection, fertility, and other purposes; and various offerings were routinely made to stone statues of cats. Entire cities were even dedicated to the worship of the cat, which was regarded as a sacred animal and a divine symbol of the Egyptian cat-goddess Bastet (also known as Ubastet, Bast, or Pasht).

The sages of ancient Egypt declared that the magickal powers and divinity of the cat served to keep eternal darkness from swallowing the world and depriving mankind of the benefits of the sun. The cat also protected the granaries and the hearth. They held more power and importance than any other animal.

Cats were so sacred to the Egyptians of old that the pharaohs forbade their export and made it illegal for any person to bring harm to a cat or kitten. To kill a cat "with malice aforethought" was punishable by death. However, if an individual accidentally killed a cat, he was subject to pay whatever fine was imposed by the priests.

According to Herodotus (an early Greek traveler in Egypt who took great interest in the Egyptian reverence for the feline), the killing of a cat was considered by the people of Egypt a crime of greater magnitude than the murder of a human being. The life of a cat was so precious that if a fire threatened a house, the first priority of the firefighters was to save the lives of the cats trapped inside. Afterwards, the rescue of the human occupants and their personal possessions would be carried out.

In the year 450 B.C., Herodotus recorded in his journal a horrific event he witnessed in the streets of Alexandria. A Roman soldier had literally been torn limb from limb by an infuriated mob of Egyptians because he had caused the death of a cherished household cat. Such happenings were said to have been common throughout Egypt. In those days, a wise man was one who took care to harm not even a single whisker of a cat!

When an Egyptian family's cat used up all of its nine lives, all members of the bereaved family would enter full mourning, traditionally shaving off their eyebrows. This was done to express their sorrow and also to show their respect for the deceased animal.

With full ceremony, the lifeless body of the cat was embalmed with various drugs, aromatic oils, and spices, then wrapped either in plain linen (if the family was poor) or in expensive multicolored strips of linen, pleated into elaborate patterns (if the family was wealthy). Next, a papier-mâché or sculptured wooden mask was placed over the cat's head. This was also carefully covered with linen and painted or decorated

with the finest of gold gilt. The mummified body was then
enclosed in a jewel-covered mummy case along with food,
bowls of milk, and even mummified mice and shrews to ensure
the cat's happiness and well-being in the afterworld. For kittens,
small coffins made of bronze were often used.

Finally, an elaborate funeral complete with solemn rites
would take place and the mummified cat would be laid out to
rest either in the famous Necropolis of Bubastis, in a family
vault, or in a cat cemetery located in any town where the rites
of Bastet were duly observed.

The exact number of mummified cats buried in the many
feline cemeteries throughout Egypt is unknown; however, it
is said to be literally in the millions. Many cat mummies have
been found wearing jewels befitting a queen, while others
have been found within the pyramids, alongside their mummified masters.

In addition to its sacredness and its connection to the worship of Bastet, the cat was regarded by the ancient Egyptians
as an extremely magickal animal. They believed that it held the
greatest of occult powers and psychic abilities. Cats could not
only see in the dark, they could also see into the future and
warn humans of impending disasters and danger . . . if they
chose to do so. Cats offered the human race magickal protection, and every Egyptian household kept them for good luck and
to keep all evil forces at bay. All cats were sacred to the goddess,
and the cats belonging to the peasantry were no less respected,
revered, and valued than those kept by the great pharaohs.

Throughout Egypt, the most unfortunate of omens was to discover the body of a dead cat. This was believed to be an indication of a grave illness, a death in the family, or some other tragedy
or catastrophic event about to occur. Such an omen could also
serve as a warning that the goddess Bastet was displeased or had
been angered in some way by the foolish actions of mortals.

When cats were first introduced into Asia, they immediately were elevated to objects of worship. Chinese and Japanese

cat-worshippers alike honored the cat by making special sacrifices to it, and in India, laws protecting cats were strictly
enforced. The divinity of the cat was evident in more than
one pagan culture; however, the magnitude and duration of
the ancient cult of the cat remained nowhere greater than in
Egypt. (Incidentally, the Hebrews—who were the mortal enemies of the cat-worshipping Egyptians—regarded the cat as
an object of contempt since it was so strongly connected to
Egyptian religion and culture. It is doubtful that it is mere coincidence that not one single reference to the cat is made in
the Bible.)

The Cat With Painted Eyes

Witch-cat of the pyramids,
The shadows of the wind-worn Sphinx
Enshroud her like a priestly robe
Of velvet lined with magick.

Painted eyes like pharaoh dreams
Invoke the spell of desert stars.
Her rings of gold and royal jewels
Enchant the night with secrets.

Witch-cat of the moon-drenched Nile
Reflects the image of Bastet.
She purrs, she strokes her fur of pitch
And dances like a goddess.

—from *Priestess and Pentacle*
by Gerina Dunwich

Bastet

According to Egyptian mythology, Bastet—a feline virgin-goddess
known as the Cat Goddess of Joy—was the daughter of Ra (the

sun god and ruler of the underworld) and the mother goddess Isis (who also ruled the sun, as well as the earth and the moon). Bastet was one of the major deities of the Egyptian pantheon. In another myth, Bastet was the firstborn daughter of the supreme creator god, Amun. She begat a lion-headed son named Mihos, whose center of worship was in the city of Bubastis.

The cat-goddess was originally worshipped in the form of a lioness (like her sister Sekhmet—a ferocious deity who represented the destructive aspects of the sun, and devoured the less-than-fortunate enemies of the sun god). By circa 1000 B.C. Bastet's guise had transformed into that of a benevolent cat. Her popularity grew to become widespread throughout Egypt, and she was often depicted in works of art as a deity possessing the body of a woman with the head of a cat (which, unsurprisingly, was the animal most sacred to her). In later Egyptian theology she took on the appearance of a cat-headed hawk, emphasizing the spirituality of the cat and symbolizing the "soaring immortal soul."

Bastet's major role was that of a deity who presided over fertility and sexuality, and she represented the benevolent aspects of the sun. She was regarded as the protectress of the North, the healer of the sick (especially children), and the patroness of motherhood. She protected the dead and decreed the success or failure of all growing things. Bastet was frequently called upon by women wishing to bear children, and by farmers in desperate need of rain. Eventually, she became a goddess linked to the sun, the moon, and the powers of love as well.

The cat goddess (whose cult lasted from circa 3200 B.C. until the end of the fourth century A.D. when the practice of paganism was officially outlawed by Theodosius I) was, for the most part, a goddess with a gentle disposition. However, like most pre-Christian goddesses, she was not without her wrath if properly provoked.

The Magick of Bastet

In contemporary witchcraft and sex-magick circles, Bastet remains one of the most popular of ancient Egyptian goddesses. She is often invoked in fertility rites and in cat-magick. Nearly all witches and pagan folk who are cat-lovers hold a special place in their hearts for Bastet.

The following spells are based on actual magickal practices of the ancient Egyptians who exalted the cat to divine status and endowed it with its ninefold life.

For protection against all opposition and evil forces, inscribe a scarab talisman with the divine image of the cat-goddess and the following words of power: "May Bastet, the great Lady of Bubastis, give protection." When the moon is full, you must anoint the talisman with three drops of frankincense oil (an oil believed since ancient times to be potent with protective magickal properties) and then wear it on a necklace, sleep with it underneath your pillow, or carry it in your pocket, purse, or special charmbag. (To increase the talisman's magickal power, touch it nine times with the tail of a live cat before applying the anointment.)

The ancient Egyptians inscribed scarabs of gold, ivory, wood, or stone with various images of, and prayers to, the goddess Bastet. Their magickal purposes included, but were not limited to: giving life and power, prosperity, truth, hunting, making rain, healing the sick or injured, promoting fertility, protecting pregnant women and children, guarding cats against snake bites, "exorcising" scorpion poison from stung cats, warding off evil spirits, and keeping temples and households safe from venomous animals.

Bastet's image, name, and sacred invocation were also engraved upon magickal wands of ivory, which were buried in tombs to keep the bodies of the dead safe from the many evils that existed in the supernatural realm and in the hereafter. It is believed that the horoscopes of the dead were engraved upon the wands as well.

To invoke the ancient power and graceful catlike presence of the goddess Bastet, inscribe her divine name nine times upon of a

cat-shaped candle (preferably one that is of a color correspond-
ing to your intent—see pages 26–27. Anoint the candle with
frankincense, lotus, or any other type of fragrant oil as you meditate upon the cat-goddess. Next, you must cast a clockwise circle for protection and then light the candle in the center of your
altar, along with a censer filled with frankincense and myrrh.
Open your heart to Bastet, fill your mind with her image, and
recite the following pagan prayer nine consecutive times:

> O great lady of Bubastis:
> She of divine feline form
> Who giveth life and power,
> I ask thee now to harken
> To my words and to my heart.
> O mistress of the oracle
> And carrier of the sacred eye:
> She who is known as
> The Lady of the East,
> I call to thee now
> With prayer and flame.
> This sacred candle burneth most bright
> In thine honor and to invoke
> Thy power and presence most divine.
> Within this circle sunwise cast
> O Goddess of Cat Enchantment
> Make thyself revealed before me.
> Praise be to Bastet!
> Praise be to Bastet!
> Praise be to Bastet!
> So mote it be.

Once you have invoked Bastet and experienced her presence
within your circle, you should speak, and at the same time visualize, what your intent is. You may also talk directly with the
goddess, using your voice or thoughts. She will hear you either
way and know what is in your heart.

Continue the ritual until the candle burns itself out (which may take several hours, depending upon the size of the candle) or until you feel that the time is right to bring the ritual to a close. Give sincere thanks, in your own words, to Bastet for her presence, protection, and favors, and then bid her farewell. Uncast the circle either by actually tracing it with a sword in a counterclockwise fashion or by visualizing its boundaries dematerializing and extinguish the candle with a snuffer or your moistened fingertips pinched together. (Many witches and pagans believe that using your breath to blow out a candle's flame after performing a spell or ritual is an insult to the gods and causes bad luck.)

Bubastis

Located on an island in the Nile Delta region of Lower Egypt, Bubastis (known today as Tel Basta) was one of the six major cities of that region, and without a doubt the most important center of the Bastet cult.

In Bubastis there stood a grand temple of red granite that housed in its inner shrine a great stone statue of the cat-goddess seated upon her throne. At its feet, priests once laid offerings of fruit, honey, meat, and exotic oils, while singing maidens danced around it with rattles and censers of fragrant incense. In the shadow of the temple's great hall, untold numbers of cats— the sacred companions of Bastet—would prowl; each adorned with necklaces, earrings, and nose rings, and all regarded as sacred as the cat goddess herself.

It is believed that a cult of Bastet was additionally centered in Upper Egypt at the Karnak temple complex; however, it was in Bubastis that an annual springtime festival of Bastet was held. Each year, more than half a million worshippers of the cat goddess would make pilgrimages by boat to this city to attend her sacred event and to receive her divine blessings. With joyous parades and an atmosphere comparable in all likelihood

Bastet was a goddess who appeared with the body of a woman and the head of a cat. She was one of the most popular deities worshipped by the ancient Egyptians. (British Museum)

to a Mardi Gras street celebration, the Bastet festival was a day of dancing, singing, feasting, drinking, and mirth making. The event was not complete, of course, without a few ritual frenzies and wild drunken orgies. At the Necropolis (Bubastis's famous cat cemetery), each year at festival time the burial of nearly 100,000 mummified cats gathered from all parts of Egypt would also take place as part of the ritual to honor the goddess.

It is said that of all the religious festivals celebrated by the Egyptians of ancient times, the springtime festival of Bastet was by far the gayest and most popular, and it had the greatest number of attendees.

Feline Deities From Around the World

Bastet, the cat-headed goddess of the ancient Egyptians, is by far the most well-known of all feline deities worshipped in pre-Christian times, and many regard her name as being almost synonymous with the words *cat goddess.* However, Bastet was not the only deity in the world (or even in ancient Egypt for that matter) who took the form of a cat, or who was associated with cats in ancient religion and myth. A number of gods and goddesses from various pantheons have been worshipped in cat form, and each has made a unique contribution to the magick, folklore, and history of pagan culture.

Another, but lesser known, cat goddess of the ancient Egyptians was Maldet. She was worshipped during the First Dynasty; however, her cult did not become as widespread as that of Bastet.

In Heracleopolis, a cat goddess called Maau (pronounced as ma-a'oo) was once worshipped. She was associated with Her-Shef, the self-created Great Father whose eyes were the sun and moon. Maau, who was also known as both Atet and Mersekhnet, was a Great Mother deity, and bore a strong resemblance to Hathor, Isis, and Neith. Like the goddess Bastet, Maau was also a slayer of Apep, the great serpent of night's darkness and adversary of the sun god.

Ra, the sun god of Heliopolis, was also represented in myth as a great cat, and in his feline form he was sometimes known as Mau. The "Great Cat who is in Heliopolis" is mentioned in the Egyptian *Book of the Dead,* which states that "the male cat is Ra himself, and he is called *Mau* by reason for the speech of the god Sa, who said concerning him: "He is like unto that which he hath made; thus his name became *Mau.*" (It is interesting to note that *mau* was also the Egyptian word for "cat.")

Whenever a solar eclipse darkened the sky, terrified Egyptians were convinced that it was caused by a great battle to the death between Ra and Apep—the gods of light and darkness, respectively. If Ra (who always transformed into a giant cat during battle) was overpowered, the sun would disappear and unending night would take its place. When the eclipse finally passed, a great celebration was held throughout the land, for the return of the sun meant that the Great Cat had once again defeated the monstrous serpent.

A cat god known as Li Shou is mentioned in the Chinese *Book of Rites.* He was worshipped by farmers in the agricultural regions of China as a benevolent deity who protected the crops by devouring destructive rats and mice. Each year after the fields had been harvested, an orgiastic festival was held and sacrifices to the cat-god were performed as a way to offer thanks and also to ensure the success of the following year's crops.

Long ago on the northern Peruvian coast, the Mochica people worshipped a feline deity called Ai Apaec. Often depicted as an old man possessing a wrinkled face, long fangs, and cat-like whiskers, he was said to have been a divine being that evolved from an ancient cat-god. In addition to being a supreme deity, Ai Apaec was the patron of farmers, fishermen, hunters, and healers, and also presided over the miracle of human reproduction.

In pre-Christian Poland, a deity in the form of a black cat and known as Ovinnik was worshipped by many farming families. Ovinnik was regarded as "the spirit of the barn" who watched over domestic animals and chased away evil-natured ghosts and mischievous fairies.

In ancient times the people of Ireland believed in the existence of a cat-god called Cairbre Cinn Cait. His name translates into "of the cat's head," and he was a deity associated with the Fir Bolg (the enemies of the Gaulish Danann people).

Scottish legend holds that the goddess of all witches was Mither o' the Mawkins. (Mawkin, or malkin, is an archaic word for the traditional witch's cat-familiar.) Interestingly, many people in Scotland once believed that goblins took the form of cats—especially in County Caithness, which literally means "county of cats."

In addition to these cat deities, many pagan gods and goddesses, who are normally depicted in humanlike form, have been known to change themselves into cats at one time or another. Examples of such deities include: the Egyptian goddess Isis; the Roman moon-goddess Diana; the Celtic mother-goddess Cerridwen; and the Greek goddesses Hecate, Artemis, and Demeter.

In Judeo-Christian myths, both the Devil and Lilith (the first wife of Adam) are often said to assume the form of black cats. The Devil in feline appearance supposedly assisted witches and warlocks of the Middle Ages in their magickal evil-doings, while Lilith in the guise of a vampiric cat sucked the blood of newborn children at night while they lay sleeping.

In Praise of Ra

Inscribed upon the walls of royal tombs in Thebes, Egypt, are the Seventy-five Praises of Ra. They are believed to date back to the nineteenth and twentieth Dynasties (approximated 2300 years ago). They were considered extremely powerful as well as sacred to the ancient Egyptians. One of the Praises is as follows:

"Praise be to thee, O Ra, exalted Sekhem, thou art the Great Cat, the avenger of the gods, and the judge of words, and the president of the sovereign chiefs and the governor of the holy Circle; thou art indeed the bodies of the Great Cat."

PAGAN GODDESSES ASSOCIATED WITH CATS

Anait (Phoenician)	Hecate (Greek)
Artemis (Greek)	Isis (Egyptian)
Bastet (Egyptian)	Liberty (Roman)
Cerridwen (Celtic)	Maau (Egyptian)
Diana (Roman)	Maldet (Egyptian)
Freya (Norse)	Mut (Egyptian)
Hathor (Egyptian)	Shasti (Indian)

PAGAN GODS ASSOCIATED WITH CATS

Ahriman (Persian)	Li Shou (Chinese)
Ai Apaec (Peruvian)	Ovinnik (Polish)
Cairbre Cinn Cait (Irish)	Ra (Egyptian)
Horus (Egyptian)	Set (Egyptian)

Cats of the Gods

Freya was the ancient Nordic goddess of love, marriage, and prosperity. A beautiful blonde-haired, blue-eyed deity who wept tears of gold, she was also a fierce warrioress. One of the many names by which she was known was the Mistress of the Cats, and it was

The goddess Freya in her chariot drawn by cats

said that the chariot in which she sat was drawn by a pair of great cats with fur blacker than the midnight sky.

In their conquest of paganism and in response to the increasing popularity of a Freya-worshipping Teutonic cult throughout northern and western Europe, the early Christians condemned Freya as an evil witch. They subsequently declared her sacred animal, the cat, to be a creature of evil, the harbinger of bad luck, the symbol of sorcery, and an animal that served the Devil.

The cat was also an animal sacred to Utgard-Loki, the fabled king of the giants. According to ancient Norse legend, his companion was a giant cat.

In one Norse myth, the mighty god Thor paid a visit to Jotunheim—the land of the ice giants, whose inhabitants asked him to prove his strength by lifting a gigantic cat up into the air. Thor attempted the great task, but even with all of his strength and godly power, he could only manage to lift one of the cat's paws off the ground. The ice giants were impressed, nonetheless, for the giant cat was actually the great, earth-encircling serpent of Midgard in feline form.

The Greek goddess Hecate, a lunar deity and the protectress of all witches, had black cats as her feline aides (in addition to black dogs). Greek mythology tells of how Hecate once changed herself into a cat in order to escape from the monster Typhon, who was slain later by the great god Zeus. Afterwards, Hecate extended special treatment to all cats and aided them in all matters related to witchcraft and the world of the occult. (This myth is responsible for one of the theories of how the cat came to be regarded as the traditional witches' familiar.)

Another goddess whose aides were black cats was Hel. In Nordic mythology, she ruled the underworld and took command of all who died, with the exception of heroes whose lives ended on the battlefield. Her realm was said to have been a sacred cave of magickal fire and rebirth, and like the goddess Hecate, Hel possessed three faces.

The cat, with its independent nature, was used as the symbol of liberty by the people of ancient Rome (and later by the French during the French Revolution of 1789). In works of art, Libertas—the Roman goddess who presided over liberty—was often shown with a scepter in one hand, a chalice in the other, and a cat lying at her feet.

THE PURRING PRIESTESS

Resplendent in her manner and form,
She prowls the temple of the night.
Of old gods and mysterious ways
Her velvet footsteps sing.

—from *Priestess and Pentacle*
by Gerina Dunwich

2

Cat-Magick

Since times most ancient, cats have been a vital part of the magickal arts and have left their mark (or should I say "claw mark") on the world of divination, folk healing, and occult sciences.

Generally, cats that are all white are connected with the practice of white (or positive) magick, while black cats are the symbol of black (or negative) magick and evil doings. Gray cats are said to be good for either positive or negative spell-craft and what is commonly referred to as gray magick, which is a blend of the two.

This correspondence of cat color to certain types of magick is traditional, but not without its exceptions. For instance, in some cultures white cats are associated with black magick and are considered to be extremely unlucky, while precisely the opposite applies to cats of the blackest fur.

Cats have long been used in the casting of spells innumerable; they have been said to assist witches in their practice of the Craft since the dawn of the Middle Ages. In many primitive systems of magick they are even used as ingredients of potion brews, aphrodisiacs, mojo charms, and all manner of magickal ointments and powders.

Although all parts of the cat are highly magickal and full of supernatural power, the body parts most popularly used by some practitioners of Santeria, Voodoo, Hoodoo, and the arts of sorcery are: whiskers, tail, eyes, claws, fur, and bones.

The majority of contemporary witches, pagans, and magicians do not use animal parts in their spells and rituals, and no true follower of the Craft of the Wise would ever think of deliberately bringing harm upon, or taking the life of, a cat or any other animal for the mere sake of creating magick. Apart from being completely unnecessary for the success of spells and the worship or invoking of the old gods, the sacrifice of life is a major violation of the Wiccan Rede, which states: "An' it harm none, do what ye will."

You will discover that some of the spells in this chapter speak of using animal parts for conjuring and enchanting; however, such spells are from olden times and have been selected for inclusion in this book solely for their historic value. They are not intended for actual use in modern times.

CAT-MAGICK

Tail and whiskers,
Claws and fur,
Spells cast by a gentle purr
Call the Moon when night is dark
And charmed by faeries on a lark.

Eyes like Witch-fire
Green and glowing
Speak with silence, quite foreknowing.
In the night your magick thrives,
Enhanced by each of your nine lives.

—from *Priestess and Pentacle*
by Gerina Dunwich

Cat Charms

In China, it is not uncommon for shopkeepers to keep live cats collared and on silken leashes as living charms to bring prosperity. It is believed that all cats attract luck, but the ones that are the oldest and ugliest attract good fortune in abundance. A good luck cat needs to be meticulously cared for and well-guarded because if it should starve to death or run away, its owner's prosperity will instantly turn into misfortune.

In Japan, figures of beckoning cats have been made from clay, porcelain, wood, or papier-mâché, and have been used since ancient times as charms for good luck, warding off pain and illness, and protection against evil. Japanese silkworm farmers are known to have used such cat charms, as well as real cats, to keep their precious, developing cocoons safe from rats and mice. Additionally, children throughout the country were kept safe from injuries and sickness by the wearing of special charms in the shape of cats.

To own or encounter a black cat was considered extremely lucky in Japan, and these animals were often kept in homes and businesses for good luck. Black cats were also held in high esteem for their supposed talismanic power to prevent or miraculously cure diseases—especially those that afflicted children.

The Japanese once believed that all long-tailed cats (unlike their native short-tailed breeds) were gifted with shape-shifting abilities. Red or pinkish-colored cats were said to possess supernatural powers and were greatly feared. According to an old Buddhist belief, a dark cat attracts gold to its master's household, while a pale cat attracts silver.

In ancient Egypt, small statues of cats, as well as figurines of the sacred cat-goddess Bastet, were popularly employed as charms to promote fertility, protect children and pregnant women, and attract good luck. They were also buried along with mummies in order to guard the dead. Egyptian cat charms were most commonly made of marble, bronze, clay, stone, glass, wood, precious stones, and all manner of metals. They were often hung on the walls and doors of houses in ancient Egypt, and their mysterious powers were called upon by both pharaoh and peasant alike. Amuletic and talismanic images of cats were engraved upon the scarabs, bracelets, and pendants of Egyptian royalty. Their tombs, as well as the tombs of their cherished cats, were frequently inscribed with prayers and invocations to the sacred goddess who possessed the head of a cat.

Egyptian women who desired to have a certain number of children placed upon the walls of their dwellings special bas-relief amulets of mother cats with the matching number of kittens. These fertility charms were empowered by daily prayers to Bastet and by anointment with sacred oils.

Farmers in the Transylvania region of central Romania once believed that if they buried a cat's body or its cremated remains in their fields, it would act as a powerful fertility charm and reward them with a bountiful crop. In many instances, such a magickal charm required that the cat be buried alive!

The use of cats in fertility rites and as fertility charms was popular in many parts of Europe during the Middle Ages. Country folks believed that cats could not only improve the yield of their crops, but that they could also prevent weeds from growing in gardens and newly ploughed fields and protect the farm against blight, storms, drought, insect plagues, and whatever magickal mischief could be brewed up by spiteful witches.

At harvest time, it was common for the paws of a cat to be mercilessly sliced off with the final swathe of the scythe. This was carried out for good luck as well as to ensure the success of the following year's plantings. Many farmers' wives in parts of Europe would also cook the cat and then serve its meat to their families for supper.

Up until the close of the eighteenth century, cats in France were burnt in bonfires to promote fertility in women, animals, and the land. Women wishing to conceive a child would leap over the flames, while farmers would force their livestock through the rising smoke. After the setting of the sun, torchlight

An illustration from *Fairy Tales by the Countess d'Aulnoy* (George Routledge and Sons, Ltd. London, 1888)

parades would wind their way through the crop fields and gardens to further improve the crops.

Fertility-promoting fire ceremonies traditionally took place annually on the Summer Solstice. The first day of summer was once believed to be the most magickal day of the entire year—a time when fairies frolicked, witches drew down the Moon, and the magickal powers of trees and flowers were at their peak.

The success or failure of a future harvest was often determined in early times by the divinatory method of dropping a live cat from the top of the bell tower of a church. If the cat landed on its feet, a good harvest was portended. If the cat landed on any other part of its body and lived, this was generally taken to mean that a difficult year for the farmers lay ahead. But if the cat died from the impact of the fall or from any bodily injuries sustained by it, this was interpreted as a truly grim omen.

To promote fertility in women, an old book devoted to Hoodoo magick suggests wearing nine cat's claws on a necklace or carrying them inside a charm-bag filled with catnip, mandrake roots, and mugwort (three herbs long-associated with fertility). This age-old connection between the cat and fertility magick undoubtedly has much to do with the feline's prolific nature.

The cat has also been used as a charm against both the Devil and those who were skilled in the art of black magick. A bone from a cat that had been unfortunate enough to be boiled alive was a gruesome, but popular, antiwitchcraft charm used in the Dutch Country of Pennsylvania. The fear of witches and the strong belief in such protective charms were believed to be the elements responsible for a widespread outbreak of cat killings that occurred in that state in 1929.

It was once common in ancient times for cats to be buried alive in the foundations of buildings. This was done to keep the structures safe from fires and to attract good fortune to the families dwelling within them. Upon occasion, this undeniably cruel method of magick would be accompanied by the ritual sacrifice of a human being—particularly a young, virginal female. In some parts of the modern world, there exist certain primitive cultures that continue this barbaric cat killing practice in the belief that it brings good luck. Even in the supposedly "civilized" United States, the intentional burials of live cats in foundations have been known to occur as late as the twentieth century! Any person capable of committing such a horrible act can only be classified as inhumane and seriously disturbed. Luckily for the feline community, this practice does not occur with any great frequency.

Long ago, many people in the rural regions of France believed that a pampered cat was the best good luck charm any family could own. If a cat was well cared for, happy, and contented, its mystical energies warded off bad luck and poverty, and attracted good fortune. Cats that were employed as living

The connection between witches and cats is evident in this illustration of an old Scottish rhyme. (BBC Hulton Picture Library)

charms were known to the French as *matagots,* which means "magickal cats."

Throughout Asia, the ancient tradition of carving pieces of jade into the shapes of cats and employing them as magickal charms to protect pregnant women is carried on in contemporary times. To ease the pains associated with childbirth, a jade cat charm is often placed over a woman's navel during delivery, while special prayers are recited and incense burned.

Many modern witches and pagans wear various cat-shaped jewelry not only to express their love for cats, but also to benefit by the jewelry's amuletic and talismanic power to stimulate or increase telepathic abilities, improve night vision, protect against evil entities, or make secret wishes come true. Cat-shaped amulets can also be worn or carried to attract beneficial vibrations into one's life. They are said to be especially favorable for all persons born under the astrological signs of Capricorn and Pisces.

Creating Magick With Cat-Shaped Candles

Cat-shaped candles come in all sizes, shapes, and colors, and can often be obtained at occult shops, gift and novelty stores, and through mail-order companies that specialize in merchandise for cat lovers. Witches who like to craft their own candles can purchase cat-shaped candle molds in shops and catalogues that sell candle-making supplies.

Whether store-bought or homemade, cat-shaped candles are potent tools of spell-craft for their very shape alone reflects the image of one of the most mysterious, magickal, and psychic of all animals. Ideally, they should always be purchased or crafted when the moon is new, waxing, or full; but never when the moon is waning. This rule applies to all candles intended for positive spell-work and deity-honoring or deity-invoking rituals.

Before lighting your cat-shaped candle, it is a good idea to consecrate it by whatever method you normally employ. Many witches and pagans traditionally prepare their new candles by placing them upon an altar, casting a circle around it, and then performing a special consecration ritual involving the four ancient elements of Earth, Air, Fire, and Water. Those who like to incorporate Native American shamanistic practices into their magick often use herbal smudging sticks to clear any negative vibrations from their candles; others feel more comfortable using simple visualization techniques combined with incantations. I suggest that you use whatever method works the best for you.

The next step, which is an equally important one, is to charge the candle with magickal energy. Using a sharp instrument like a nail or the point of a knife carefully carve into the wax of the candle whatever magickal symbols, words, or runes you feel are appropriate for your spell-work. As you do this, be sure to concentrate upon your intent. If you choose not to carve anything upon your candle, you can simply hold it in your hands instead and meditate upon your intent for as long as you feel is necessary.

Next, anoint the candle with three drops of oil. You can use either a store-bought or a homemade oil; however, make sure you use one that magickally corresponds to your intent. For instance, an oil associated with love (such as rose) should be employed for candles used in any type of love magick; an oil associated with wealth (such as pine) should be employed for candles used in money-drawing spells, and so forth. (Note: You will find a complete list of essential oils and their magickal properties in my book, *Magick Potions,* published by Citadel Press, 1997.)

Bastet Candle

A candle in the shape of this deity is ideal for use in spells and rituals involving fertility, love enchantment, protection, and all manner of cat-magick. Place a lighted Bastet candle on an altar to honor or invoke the powers of the ancient Egyptian cat-goddess. This is also an appropriate candle to use for feline funeral rites and for ensuring that the soul of a deceased kitten or cat is guarded in the afterlife.

Cat-Angel Candle

Winged cat-angels have become a popular design in recent times. Place one of these adorable candles on your altar for spiritual guidance, enlightenment, and protection against harm and all manner of evil. You can also place a cat-angel candle next to your bed to keep you safe from nightmares and psychic attacks while you are sleeping. Burn a cat-angel candle to magickally protect your cat against bewitchment, injuries, sickness, and theft, as well as to safely guide a lost or runaway cat back to its home.

Kitten Candle

A candle in the shape of a kitten can be used in spells and rituals to symbolize innocence, new beginnings, growth, and happiness. It can also be ritually burned to aid in the healing of sick or injured kittens, or to ensure the safe delivery of newborn kittens.

Black Cat Candle

In the ancient art of candle magick, the color black is often associated with death and the practices of cursing, hexing, and jinxing. However, black candles can also be used to break curses, banish negative energies, and cast spells that involve endings. A candle in the shape of a black cat can be used to represent a cat with black fur in spells utilizing image magick, and in England (where the black cat is regarded as an animal of good luck) such candles are often used in spells to break streaks of bad luck.

White Cat Candle

To aid meditation or promote the powers of clairvoyance, burn upon your altar a white cat candle anointed with three drops of essential oil of either acacia or nutmeg (two magickal oils that have long been associated with both meditation and psychic powers). In candle magick, the color white represents prophecy, purification, spirituality, truth, and wholeness. A candle in the shape of a white cat can be used to represent a cat with white fur in spells utilizing image magick. It can also be employed to attract good luck, consecrate a ritual space, and strengthen the psychic and spiritual bond between a witch and her cat-familiar.

Green Cat Candle

The energies associated with this type of candle can be used in spells to aid an injured or sick cat's healing process, as well as to promote fertility in female cats. They can also be highly beneficial for any type of ritual work concerning cats who make their homes out in the wild. For humans, a green cat candle can be used in spells to attract money, overcome feelings of jealousy or greed, and restore the balance of the yin and yang energies.

Red Cat Candle

The traditional magickal properties long associated with red candles include courage, magnetism, love, passion, and willpower. For cats, a red candle in a cat's image can be a powerful tool for healing, especially when burned in spells to improve health, strengthen a weak or aged body, or treat blood-related diseases, such as feline leukemia (a cancer of the blood in which the red cells are destroyed). Additionally, it can be used to help ensure a cat's safe and successful mating.

The names and addresses of several mail-order companies that carry cat-shaped candles can be found in the Resources section at the back of this book. For a more complete listing of shops and catalogues that carry a full line of magickal candles, read *The Wicca Source Book* by Gerina Dunwich, Citadel Press.

(The New York Public Library Picture Collection)

Spell to Change Into a Cat

The following is a curious shape-shifting spell that hails from seventeenth century Scotland. According to the testimony of Isabel Gowdrie (a Scottish Witch-Queen who was tried for sorcery in the year 1662), the thrice-repeated recitation of these words could enable her and those in her coven to physically transform themselves into cats:

> I shall goe intill ane catt,
> With sorrow, and sych,
> And a blak shott;
> And I shall goe in the Devil's name,
> Ay while I come home againe.

Loosely translated, this incantation means: "I shall transform into any cat with sorrow and sigh and a black shot. And I shall transform in the Devil's name until I return to my own shape." Occult lore holds that human-to-cat transformation can occur up to nine times during a witch's lifetime. This is obviously based on the old notion that all cats possess nine lives.

Baldwin's sixteenth-century book, *Beware of the Cat,* reinforces this belief by stating, "It was permitted to a Witch to take on her catte's body nine times."

It was believed that witches turned themselves into cats in order to roam the darkness of night unobserved, meet with the Devil, steal their neighbors food and possessions, and curse their enemies with bad luck. Sometimes witches became cats merely for the amusement of it, but on Sabbat nights they transformed their physical shapes to avoid being identified or followed while en route to and from the Black Mass.

Both female and male witches (or warlocks, as they were called by witch-hunters during the Inquisition) supposedly possessed the power to take on the shape of a cat if they so desired. However, the magickal art of cat-transformation was associated mostly with women. For male witches the animal of choice for transformation was more commonly a black dog.

When a witch in the magickally assumed shape of a cat was ready to change back into human form, all she needed to do was recite three times the following magickal formula of ritual transformation used by the aforementioned seventeenth-century sorceress Isabel Gowdrie and members of her coven:

> Catt, catt, God send thee a blak shott.
> I am in a catte's likeness just now,
> Bot I shall be in a woman's likeness ewin now.
> Catt, catt, God send thee a blak shott.

Cats and the Evil Eye

In the Middle Ages it was a common belief throughout many parts of Europe that some cats (especially black ones) possessed the power of the evil eye and could bring harm or death to both humans and animals with a mere glance. They could also turn the living into stone if they fancied it.

In many rural villages and cities alike, the fearful and superstitious routinely burned alive untold numbers of cats in an effort to protect themselves against these "demonic creatures" and the misfortune, illness, and death they were thought to cause.

In addition to possessing the evil eye, it was also believed that cats (as well as other pets and livestock) could themselves be bewitched by the evil eye of humans who were born with the so-called "Devil's gift." To counter this diabolical supernatural threat, many magickal spells and prayers for the cat's protection were devised.

One old, and extremely popular, method involved the use of small round shells (such as cowries). These would be securely attached to the animal's collar after being blessed by prayers and sprinkled with holy water. The more shells that were used, the less chance of the cat becoming bewitched. A collar that was made entirely of cowrie shells was believed by the superstitious to offer a cat the greatest protection against the evil eye.

Good Luck Cat Spell

A simple magickal spell to bestow prosperity and good luck upon a loved one, according to Thai legend, is to present that person with a gift in the form of a chartreuse-eyed korat cat.

The *korat* (an unrecognized breed of cat that hails from the Korat Plateau of Siam) is believed by many to be extremely magickal and lucky. In the country of Thailand it is known as *si-sawat* (which literally translates to "color-prosperity" and refers to the korat's yellowish-green eyes and their power to bestow a prosperous life upon the cat's human master or mistress). It is an animal that is held in very high esteem.

Good-Luck Cat Spell 2

An old witch's spell from Brittany is based on the folk belief that hidden in the tail of every pure black cat is a single, and highly magickal, white hair.

To create magick that will attract an abundance of good luck into your life, you must find the white hair, pluck it from the cat's tail while reciting the following incantation, and then keep the hair in a safe place (such as in a mojo bag or witch-bottle):

> Cat of ebony,
> Black as night,
> Bring good luck
> By pluck of white!

A word of caution: It is said that if the black cat should scratch you when you pull the hair from its tail, you will be destined to become the recipient of bad luck instead of good.

A Spell to Win at Cards

Many old-time riverboat gamblers once believed that good luck at any type of card game was guaranteed if you stroked a cat's tail nine times—a magickal method popular in Hoodoo folk magick of the southern United States. While doing so, your intent must be visualized and the following incantation recited, either silently or aloud:

> Three strokes are magick;
> Nine are divine.
> Cards be enchanted;
> Good luck be mine!

Black Cat Money Spell

In the Middle Ages, men and women who sought to increase their wealth through the magickal aid of sorcerers were often instructed to carry out the following spell at night when the moon was in its waxing phase:

Take a lifeless cat that is all black in color; cover each of its eyes with a black bean, and then bury the cat, along with a gold piece, deep in the soil of Mother Earth.

If your faith in this spell is true, then you shall never be without money. But take care never to work such a spell when the moon is on the wane or you shall find yourself cursed with poverty for the rest of your days!

A Potion for Lovers

In days of yore, the brewing of amatory potions (also known as philtres) was a popular pastime of most witches, and many made their living by concocting magickal potions for the lovelorn.

One of the most famous of all love potions from yesteryear (thanks to the poet William Butler Yeats) is the black cat love potion. This romance-inspiring philtre called for the liver to be

Chere Minette (Grandville)

removed from a black cat, dried, and ground with a mortar and pestle, then mixed together with black tea. When brewed in a black teapot and drunk by the man or woman of one's desires, it was guaranteed to inspire loving feelings in the most magickal of ways.

To Prevent Straying

Folk magick has long been used to prevent cats from straying far from home, and many spells have been designed for this purpose. Several curious examples follow:

Stroke the cat's fur while it gazes up into the chimney, or allow it to see its reflection in a looking glass. Another method calls for having a tiny bit of sugar on the cat's tongue at nine o'clock on a Friday morning. (Friday is a day sacred to Freya— a goddess associated with cats.)

How these particular spells originated and what exactly makes them work are indeed a mystery. But these, and others, have been used by witches for centuries to keep cats from running away from home or becoming lost while out prowling the night.

Protection Against Changelings

According to pagan folklore, there exist certain types of wicked fairies that delight in stealing human infants from their cribs and leaving in their place an undesirable creature that is known as a changeling. Changelings are believed to be unwanted fairy children or the half-mortal offsprings of both human and fairy parents. They are said to possess a strange appearance or be grotesquely deformed. Often, they are in poor physical health and do not live very long lives.

In olden times, a special magickal charm was devised to protect newborn babies from being stolen by fairies and replaced with a changeling. It consisted of the hair of a black cat (an animal greatly feared by most fairies) and a white feather tied together on a red-colored ribbon. In order to be effective, the charm needed to be enchanted and then worn around the neck of the child for a whole year and a day.

Bewitchment and Possession

To cure a cat that has been bewitched, make the animal walk three times in a counterclockwise circle. According to occult tradition, this will break the spell of any sorcerer. Another bewitchment-breaking method consists of the sprinkling of salt around the cat in an unbroken counterclockwise circle.

To release a cat from a sorcerer's spell, you must mark the sign of the cross upon its back. This method was popular in the Middle Ages.

The simple act of calling a witch-cat or a demon-cat by its true name is believed by many to render it powerless, but to kill it is to run the risk of becoming possessed by it. A person who dares to kill such a cat can, however, avoid falling victim to supernatural possession by eating a bit of the slain animal's flesh, according to occult folklore.

Rain Spells

In times of drought, many primitive people employed the cat as a magickal charm to make rain. Numerous methods were used, including bathing a cat in a water-filled earthenware pan; dunking a cat in a pool of water; tossing a cat into a river and then forcing it to swim back to the bank while female villagers splash in the water after it; and carrying a cat three times clockwise around a field and then drenching the cat with water from bamboo squirts while special rain-making prayers are chanted.

In Sumatra (and in other lands as well), black cats were the animals of choice for rainmaking. Spell-casters believed that, by the powers of sympathetic magick, the cat's dark color would cause the sky to grow dark with rain-bearing clouds.

Another rain-producing ritual of ancient times called for a cat-shaped stone to be anointed with the fresh blood of a properly sacrificed fowl and then enchanted with fragrant incense and magickal incantations.

In Great Britain during the Middle Ages, it was commonly believed that witches could raise storms by drawing a cat through a fire, christening the cat (i.e., giving it a name, as in a baptism ceremony), and then casting it into the waters of the ocean. Sometimes various body parts of a human corpse would be tied to the cat's body, especially if the spell was black magick intended to raise a storm at sea for the sinking of ships. (In seventh-century England, an ecclesiastical law against raising storms by "invoking fiends" was passed. A century later, the same crime was made punishable by death!)

To calm a storm, witches of old Ireland would often place a live cat underneath a metal cooking pot as soon as the rain began falling. (Witches' cat-familiars were seldom ever used for such a purpose; instead, ordinary housecats or stray alley cats were employed.) Only after the wet weather subsided would the cat be allowed its freedom.

The strong and ancient connection between cats and the workings of rain-magick is responsible for the numerous weather-related omens involving cats that have survived into contemporary times (see pages 99–101).

Spells for the Eyes

Cat-magick to heal afflictions of the eyes and cure blindness has been around since ancient times. In many parts of the world, the tail of a pure white cat is still used as a powerful charm to restore sight to the blind. It is rubbed across the eyes while a special incantation is recited.

The simple act of stroking the tail of a black cat is believed by some folks in Great Britain (where black cats have always been regarded as the bringers of good luck) to work as a spell

to ensure good eyesight in humans. It is also reputed to prevent
or cure eye irritation.

According to E. Topsell's *Historie of Four-Footed Beasties* (first
published in London in 1658), physical blindness in humans
can be cured by the following unorthodox prescription that
more closely resembles a witch-doctor's spell: "Take the head
of a black cat, which hath not a spot of another colour in it,
and burn it to powder in an earthen pot, leaded or glazed
within; then take this powder, and, through a quill, blow it
thrice a day into thy eye; and if in the night any heat do
thereby annoy thee, take two leaves of an oke, wet in cold
water, and bind them to the eye, and so shall all pain flie away,
and blindness depart, although it hath oppressed thee a whole
year; and this medicine is approved by many physicians both
elder and later."

In Cornwall (as well as in other parts of England), local
witches and folk healers were known to use cat-magick to cure
sties. This was usually accomplished by plucking a hair from the
tail of a black tomcat on the first night of the new moon and
then rubbing it nine times across the sty while repeating an
incantation such as: "I poke thee, I don't poke thee, I toke the
queff that's under thee. Oh, qualy way; oh qualy way."
Sometimes the entire tail of the cat would be utilized in the
spell (often while still attached to the cat), especially if the swell-
ing of the eyelid was severe.

Anti-Itching Spell

A strange cat-spell designed to cure any kind of itch was said
to have been used by some English witches during the Middle
Ages. It called for a black cat to be whirled thrice around the
head of a left-handed man. Nine drops of blood drawn from
the tail of the cat and the ashes of nine charred barleycorns
were then mixed together to form a magickal ointment.
However, in order for this ointment to be truly effective, a

witch needed to apply it to the itch with a gold wedding ring and then walk three times counterclockwise around the patient while invoking the Father, the Son, and the Holy Ghost.

Treasure Spell

An old spell from the rural regions of France calls for a black cat to be tied to a place where five roads come together. At the first bell of the witching hour (midnight), the cat must be set free. It is then obligated, according to occult lore, to immediately lead the witch or magician to the hidden treasure that he or she seeks.

Second Sight

To gain the power of second sight, according to an archaic spell, mix the eyes of a black cat with the gall of a man. This supposedly acts as a magickal charm for clairvoyance when carried in a mojo bag. If the bag is placed underneath the pillow at night, it reputedly brings prophetic dreams to the sleeper.

To acquire the supernatural ability to see demons with the naked eye, according to the Jewish Talmud: "Find and burn the placenta of the first litter of a black cat (which must have been one of its mother's first litter), then beat it to a powder and rub it into the eyes."

In parts of Scotland, an ancient cat-sacrificing ritual called the Taigheirm ("the cry of cats") was believed to endow a human being with the gift of second sight, and it was practiced well into the eighteenth century. It always commenced at the witching hour (midnight) between a Friday and a Saturday, and it lasted for four days and nights. Those who participated in it were required to dress in black attire and fast throughout the entire ritual. It was equally important for all of the sacrificial cats used to be pure black.

After being dedicated to the Devil, the cats would be tortured in a slow, agonizing fashion and then put on a spit, one at a time, and roasted alive in one of the most inhumane fashions imaginable. Many times throughout the ritual, infernal spirits in feline form would materialize and their unearthly cries would merge with the shrieks and howlings of the sacrificial cats to create what could only be described as a hellish harmony. Eventually a monstrous supernatural cat would appear from out of the shadows of the night and attempt to frighten and distract the leader of the ritual to the point of bringing the sacrificial rite to an abrupt halt. But if the sacrificer of the cats was intrepid and able to keep the ritual going for the required length of time without falling victim to exhaustion or the intimidating threats of the great hell-born cat, he would be granted the gift of second sight for the remainder of his life—but only after demanding from the invoked cat-spirits the reward for his feline sacrifice.

Cats as Tools of Black Magick

In the wicked world of black magick (which should not be confused with the benevolent and positive magickal practices of contemporary Wiccans), cats have always played an important role; not only as witch's imp (or familiar), but as a magickal charm as well.

In the late sixteenth century, John Fian (the most famous of all of Scotland's witches) and his coven were accused of attempting to sink the royal ship of King James VI and Queen Anne as they sailed from Scotland to Denmark. It is believed that these witches produced a great storm at sea by tying a christened cat to a dismembered human corpse and tossing it into the North Sea while reciting evil magickal chants. Although a violent storm did manifest, no harm fell upon the royal couple because their faith in God was said to have been stronger than the will of Fian and his coven.

In Vodoun black magick, it is believed that enemies near and far can easily be cursed with bad luck, illness, or death by magickal charms fashioned from the whiskers of cats. It is not uncommon to find such charms of sorcery in many of the occult shops throughout the southern regions of the United States, particularly in and around New Orleans—a city with a strong connection to the magickal practices of both Voodoo and Hoodoo.

Another strange account of cat-sorcery centers around the untimely deaths of the two young sons of the Earl and Countess of Rutland. In the year 1618, an elderly witch who publicly proclaimed her hatred for the Countess and her family confessed in a court of law that she had stolen a glove from one of the Countess's sons. When the moon was right, she boiled the glove in a cauldron of water and then rubbed it against the fur of her familiar—a black cat with the most evil of powers. With the recitation of special magickal words, she was then able to bring illness and death to the noble children.

Additionally, she admitted to placing a curse of infertility upon the Countess so that the now-childless woman would never be able to bring another son or daughter into the world. This act of malevolence was carried out by the stroking of the black cat's belly with feathers taken from the Countess's bed. It did not take long for the court to find the old woman guilty of murder by bewitchment, and she was executed on the gallows at Lincoln, England. No mention was ever made as to the fate of the black cat accomplice.

Long ago in southern Slavonia, a cruel magickal method was employed by men who made their living as thieves. It called for a cat to first be blinded and then cast into a fire until its body was reduced to charred ashes. After cooling, the ashes would be gathered in the light of the moon and stored in a special charm-bag until they were ready to be used.

When engaging in an act of robbery, the thief would cast a pinch of the cat's ashes over the person whom he was robbing in order to put them under his spell. The ashes and their mysterious powers were believed to give the thief the ability to successfully complete his crime and escape without being caught or harmed in any way.

Many old grimoires (books of magick) speak of sorcerers from ancient times who crafted magickal candles from the grease and fat of black tomcats. Known as a "Dead Man's Candle" because its wick was fashioned from the hair of a corpse, it was placed between the fingers of a hanged criminal's right hand (which was required to be severed during a lunar eclipse) and used as an evil charm. It was said to possess the power to put its victims into a trancelike state—usually so that they could be easily robbed of their money and valuables. A "Dead Man's Candle" was regarded as a powerful tool of black magick and was used by only the most evil of sorcerers.

To conjure demons, according to an old book written about cat-magick, a large cast-iron cauldron of water must be brought to a boil at a crossroads when the night is still and moonless. Into the boiling water a black cat must be dropped, and this will cause a number of demonic entities to materialize before long. If the spell is carried out as directed, it is said that the demons will grant the desires of the sorcerer (no matter what they may be) in exchange for the cat.

In Great Britain and colonial America, it was believed that cats were frequently used by witches and warlocks to carry out such dastardly deeds as killing farmers' livestock, bringing infertility to women, turning milk sour, raising storms of the most destructive fury, sucking out the life breath from babies and small children, and ruining crops by bringing down plagues of insects.

In 1699, three hundred children from Mohra, Sweden, were accused of practicing witchcraft. They supposedly testified in court that the Devil had presented each of them with a demon in the form of a kitten, and its main function was to steal food for them that would then be used as offerings to the Lord of Hell. As a result, fifteen of the three hundred children were put to death and thirty-six were punished by whippings at church every Sunday for an entire year (the same children every week).

During the Inquisition (or Burning Times as many modern witches refer to this dark and bloody period in history), the Church was convinced that cats not only possessed evil powers and served the needs of witches and other enemies of God, but that Cats were full-fledged agents of Satan, and sometimes even the Devil himself in disguise. (The Knights Templars were accused in the fourteenth century of worshipping the Devil in the form of a black cat.) Interestingly, there exist numerous legends about black cats leaping out of the fire when witches and warlocks alike were put to their fiery deaths at the stake!

Santeria, a practice similar to Voodoo, originated in West Africa and was brought to the Americas in the slave trade. It is not uncommon for black magick to be used by some of its practitioners (Santeros), and one of the animals routinely utilized in their sorcery is the cat.

One particularly evil Santeria potion for bringing an enemy's life to a violent end calls for a black cat to be tortured, boiled alive, and then buried in the ground for one whole day and night. When the sun rises the cat is unearthed, and into a cauldron are added three of its bones, seven phalanx bones from the little fingers of seven corpses (along with a bit of dust from each of their graves), garlic, pepper, and rum. The smoke from a cigar is blown upon the cauldron and after curing overnight in a forest, the potion is ready to be used.

Magickal Herbs and Cats

When one associates cats with herbs, the first plant that comes to mind is almost always catnip. And this is not without good reason, for the aroma released by this perennial herb of the mint family has an intoxicating and even powerful aphrodisiac effect on the majority of felines (both domestic and wild). Anyone who has ever witnessed a cat "getting high" on catnip could even say that its effects are next to magickal.

Catnip has long been employed by witches in all forms of cat-magick, and it is an herb popularly used in sleeping potions.

It is also sacred to all pagan gods and goddesses who manifest in the form of a cat or other feline.

Catnip toys, when ritually charged with magickal power, make excellent protective amulets for your cat-familiars. Catnip potions are ideal for use in magickal fluid condensers, washes, libations, Sabbat brews, and invocations of the Water element when performing cat-oriented spells and rituals.

Catnip Potion

To make a magickal catnip potion (which also serves as an effective nightcap), pour one and one-half cups of spring water into a small cauldron or tea kettle. Bring to a boil. Pour the water over one teaspoon of either freshly cut or dried catnip leaves and flowering tops, and then allow the potion to steep for approximately twenty minutes. Sweeten with a bit of honey or sugar if you should so desire, always being sure to stir in a clockwise direction to attract good luck and positive energies. (Stirring in a counterclockwise direction is said to attract the opposite.)

A word of caution: Although catnip potion is not poisonous, some sources warn that it should not be consumed by pregnant women.

Another herb with an intoxicating effect on most cats is valerian. Under the astrological influence of the planet Mercury (according to Culpepper), valerian is used by witches in a variety of magickal ways. The most popular usage of this herb, however, is in the brewing of sleeping potions and the making of dream pillows designed for calming the nerves and inducing relaxation and sleep.

According to Sipontius, "The root of the herb valerian (commonly called *Phu*) is very like to the eye of a Cat, and wheresoever it groweth, if Cats come thereunto, they instantly dig it up, for the love thereof, as I myself have seen in mine own Garden, and not only once, but often, even then when I had caused it to be hedged or compassed round about with thornes, for it smell-eth marvellous like to a Cat."

Ruled by the planet Mars and under the influence of the element of Fire, the herb known as rue was used throughout the Middle Ages as a protective herbal amulet against witches and their familiars. This may be one reason that cats seem to dislike this unpleasant-smelling, evergreen perennial shrub to this very day!

According to Pliny, "To keep Cats from hunting of Hens, they use to tie a little Rew [rue] under their wings, and so like-wise from Dove coates, if they set it in the windows, they dare not approach unto it for some secret in nature."

A passage from the book, *A Greene Forest* (published in the year 1567), reads: "There is also a kinde thereof called the wild Cat, which of all things is annoyed with the smell of Rue and the Almond leafe, and is driuen [driven] away with that sooner then with any other thing."

The following garden plants are poisonous or dangerous to cats: andromeda, boxwood, daphne, foxglove, lily-of-the-valley, monkshood, and privet.

The following houseplants are poisonous or dangerous to cats: azalea, bittersweet, crown of thorns, dumb cane (Diefenbachia), elephant ear, English ivy, holly, hydrangea, Jerusalem cherry, lantana, laurel, mistletoe, oleander, philodendron, pine needles, poinsettia, rhododendron, sheep laurel, and snow-on-the-mountain.

Cat Divination

Since early times, the cat has been used by diviners in many parts of the world to make predictions about the future. The art and practice of divination by the behavior and actions of cats is called felidomancy (which is Latin for "divination by felines"). It is a form of zoomancy (divination by the observation of animal behavior); however, it should not be confused with the method known as apantomancy, which draws omens from chance meetings with animals or birds (a black cat crossing one's path, for example).

Cat divination can be traced back to ancient Egypt, where the feline was deified and worshipped for many centuries. Special cats, adorned with precious jewels and magickal symbols, were used in a variety of ways by temple priests and royal diviners to look into the future, the present, and even the past. Cat divination was especially important when it concerned the fates of the pharaohs and even Egypt herself.

In ancient times, felidomancy was a practice popular not only in Egypt, but in Persia (now called Iran), Rome, Greece, Northern Europe, India, Phoenicia (now Syria and Lebanon), China, and Japan. By the dawn of the Middle Ages, cat divination was widespread throughout Europe and the British Isles.

Using the behavior of a cat to predict the weather is perhaps the oldest and most common form of felidomancy. It is still in practice in modern times, especially in rural regions where many folks continue to subscribe to the old traditional ways and beliefs of the generations before them. In the United States, cat divination is most popular in the South and in the Ozarks. However, remnants of felidomancy in the form of common weather omens can still be found just about everywhere (see pages 99–101`), even in large metropolitan areas like New York, Los Angeles, and Chicago. For additional information and detailed examples of felidomancy, see the section on Cat Omens and Superstitions.

Sometimes dreams in which a cat or cats are featured can be highly prophetic in nature, and many diviners take great stock in their dreams, using them as tools to gain an insight to the unknown and things yet to come. For more information about cat divination using dreams, see the section on Cat Dreams and What They Mean.

White Cat Marriage Divination

If you are a woman who has been proposed to but are unsure whether or not you should marry the gentleman, the following divination method (popular in days gone by, and known as "leaving it to the cat") may help you to make up your mind.

Take three hairs from the tail of a white cat with not a spot of any other color anywhere upon it and put them in a folded piece of paper. Place it underneath your doorstep at the witching hour (midnight) and recite the following incantation:

> Three hairs from a cat of white
> Beneath the door I place tonight.
> When the morning sun shines bright
> Tell me if my suitor's right.

In the morning, unfold the paper with care and examine the hairs. If they are found to cross each other, this indicates that you should accept the marriage proposal. If the hairs do not cross, your best bet would be to turn it down.

Spell to Keep a New Cat From Running Away From Home

This simple, yet effective, spell has been used by witches for centuries to keep a new cat from running away from home. When the Moon is new, rub the cat's paws in butter, and then sharpen its claws on the outside of the chimney.

Invisibility Spells

The following spell was used in ancient times by ceremonial magician Albertus Magnus. It called for the severed ear of a black cat to be boiled in the milk of a black sow while a special magickal incantation was recited. When placed over the thumb, the enchanted cat's ear was believed to impart the power of invisibility upon the magician who wore it.

The ancients also believed that the head of a cat was potent with magickal powers that could be used for either good or evil purposes. Eating a cat's head while it was still warm supposedly

A warlock (male witch) rides his feline familiar to the Witches' Sabbat. (Illustration from Ulrich Molitor's *Hexen Meysterey*, sixteenth-century)

could make a man or a woman invisible if they first recited the correct incantation. However, any person who consumed a cat's head was said to be risking madness by doing so. This was because the body of the cat belonged to God, but its head belonged to the Devil, according to an old legend.

In old Ireland, practitioners of the once-forbidden arts of wizardry and enchantment believed that a special bone from a black cat could give a human being mastery over the laws of nature that prevented the attainment of invisibility at will. To obtain such a powerful, and highly-prized, magickal charm, a black cat of either gender needed to be boiled alive at midnight during a full moon. Afterwards, the animal's bones had to be carefully separated and cleaned. The procedure to find the bone of invisibility was as follows: While gazing at his reflection in a looking glass, the magician would place the cat's bones, individually, within his mouth until he came upon the one which made his reflection disappear from sight.

3

Cat Dreams and What They Mean

According to dream-analysis books, the most common animal to appear in our dreams is the cat. It is representative of the imaginative power of the unconscious, and often serves as a symbol for intuitive feminine wisdom as well.

THE DREAM-CAT

When nighttime spins her darkened web
And silence chants her charmed refrain,
The dream-cat comes on moonlight paws
With starbright eyes of magick.
In mirthful dreams and mares of night
She dwells and casts enchantments well;
Secret omens she does bring
To those versed in her ways.

Her graceful shadow whispers of
A thousand ancient gods divine.
Gaze into her mystic eyes . . .
Behold another world.

—from *Priestess and Pentacle*
by Gerina Dunwich

Humans have always been fascinated by dreams and their hidden meanings and messages. Dreams can bestow inspiration upon us, or terror, and they can be a simple, natural means to peek into the future or tap into the realms of the unknown. Dreams can be magickal, and if we open our minds to the power of our dream symbols, they can take us on wondrous journeys beyond the limits of the three-dimensional world in which our physical bodies dwell.

It is a natural event for us to awaken from a dream (or a nightmare) and ponder its meaning. People have been doing this since the dawn of time. The number of dream symbols and their combinations are infinite, and some are of a prophetic nature, while others are not. Every dream is a unique experience, and the same dream symbol may hold different meanings for different persons.

But if a dream or nightmare is one that involves cats in one way or another, what is it trying to make us aware of? What exactly is involved in the process of dream analysis, and how can our dreams be used as effective tools of divination? Within this chapter the answers to these questions, as well as others, shall be revealed.

Many dream analysts suggest that the meaning that lies within a cat-dream may depend upon the way the individual perceives the cat. For instance, to a person with a real-life fear of cats (ailurophobia), the appearance of a cat within their dream may actually be symbolic of that person's own inner fears, or perhaps even a fear connected with a feminine aspect. (This could apply to one's mother, for example. Or it could also, regardless of the dreamer's gender, be linked to his or her feminine side.)

The various aspects of the feminine, like all else in the universe, possess both positive and negative qualities. When a dream-cat is in league with the positive side of the feminine, the dream may be indicating such things as creativity, fertility, the possibility of new growth within a certain area of your life, and so forth. The femininity of the cat symbol also links it to the energy and wisdom of Mother Nature, the unconscious psyche, the mysteries of the Goddess, and the perpetual cycle of birth, death, and rebirth.

On the other hand, when a dream-cat is in league with the negative side of the feminine, the dream may be revealing the "catty" side of one's personality, an imbalance of yin energy, or destructive tendencies. (Most psychologists agree that repressed femininity often surfaces in our dreams—as well as in our real lives—in a manner most negative.)

Cats and Christmas

Long ago, people in Germany once believed that a dream involving cats and Christmas was a warning from the gods. It indicated that a serious illness would strike within the course of a year.

Black Cats

A black cat in a dream can denote either good luck or misfortune, depending upon which you associate a black cat with. In some parts of the world, black cats are regarded as luck-bringers, while in other places they are feared and linked to omens of bad luck and evil.

Likewise, a black cat is often associated with the traditional sorceress and her powers. If one associates them with the dark forces of evil, then the dream may well serve as a warning to watch out for evil influences, the presence of negativity, or anything that is generally regarded as being bad. The symbol of the black cat may also point to the dreamer's own hidden dark side, or warn against an impending harm.

However, if an individual associates the black cat and the witch with the Earth-honoring Craft of the Wise (Wicca, Neo-Paganism, and so forth), the dream symbol would then be of a more positive nature, representing perhaps the benevolent magickal powers, healing energies, great wisdom, and sacredness of the Divine Feminine.

It is said to be a sign of good luck when witches dream about a black cat, but a bad omen for those who are not of the Craft. According to the old occult method of dream analysis and divination that proposes dreams reveal precisely the opposite, to dream about a black cat on a Friday the thirteenth (supposedly the unluckiest day of the year) would actually be the luckiest dream that anyone could ever hope to experience!

Cats' Eyes

A dream involving cats' eyes is said to be representative of either the unconscious or the anima (the female half of the soul or mind, symbolically connected with the feminine elements of Earth and Water). Cats' eyes are mysterious, mystical, and incredibly magickal by nature. They are believed by some to be the windows to an enchanted fairyland or spirit-world, and they are often linked with the moon (another symbol of femininity, the Goddess, and the witch).

Cats That Teach Us

Cats that appear in our dreams to teach us or warn us of something often accomplish their mission through any of the old figures of speech that are attached to them. Obvious meanings can be found in such phrases as: "letting the cat out of the bag," "playing a game of cat and mouse," being a "copycat," living "under the cat's paw," and so forth. When attempting to inter-pret a dream, especially one that may appear vague or especially puzzling, all possibilities must be taken into consideration.

Dreaming of Being a Cat

To dream that you are a cat is indicative of a transformation. Changes, such as those that occur in one's lifestyle, career, rela-tionships, and so forth, can be either good or bad, depending upon the final outcome of the dream. If, as a cat in your dream, you encounter unpleasant experiences but the dream has a happy ending, it may be interpreted that a recent change, or one soon to transpire, will be accompanied by difficulties or set-backs. However, the end result will be a positive one for you.

Kittens

Kittens are cute and cuddly, and when they appear in our dreams they symbolize new beginnings, a period of (or need for) growth, innocence, and playfulness, or a desire to return to childhood or be nurtured. Kittens as a negative dream symbol may stand for immaturity, vulnerability, annoying "kittenish" behavior, turning a "blind eye" to something (newborn kittens are often thought of as being "blind" until their eyes open). They may also indicate a state of great mental confusion or emotional turmoil (hence the old expression, "I nearly had kittens!"). To witness a mother cat giving birth to kittens is symbolic of the birth of something new. For a woman, it may also indicate a desire to bear children, or it may serve as an omen connected with pregnancy.

Cat Attacks

It is said that when a cat claws at you in a dream or in a night-mare, this is a hidden warning that you will soon become the victim of a betrayal. The same applies to all dreams in which you are bitten by a cat or pursued by it like prey.

White Cats

Although white cats are generally considered to be the bringers of good luck in most parts of the world, when they show up in a dream it usually indicates that a loss of some kind will soon take place if you do not act with care.

Sick or Injured Cat

To dream about a sick, injured, or dying cat may foretell emotional stress, illness, or a great disappointment. To see a dead cat in one's dream is generally thought of as a bad sign, although some say that death is actually a dream symbol for transformation and new beginnings. To dream about killing a cat may indicate repressed hostility toward a mother or other female authority figure, or sibling rivalry with a sister. It may also express the dreamer's resentment of his or her feminine side or even indicate a repression of intuitive powers or creativity.

Cats With More Than One Tail

A cat that possesses more than one tail is a very magickal and powerful dream symbol. (Incidentally, in Irish folklore there exist double-tailed and ten-tailed cats possessing the greatest of magickal powers.) Such a dream may symbolize the increase of the dreamer's spiritual energy. Cats' tails are essential for balance; therefore, to dream about either a tailless cat or the cutting off of a cat's tail is an indication that something in your life is out of balance. If you are unsure of what the cause of the imbalance is, possible clues can be found in the other symbols in the dream.

A Cat Catching a Mouse

Success, swiftness, or the ability to make quick decisions is said to be denoted by the dream of a cat catching a mouse—

a pastime relished by most predatory felines. To dream of a cat engaged in its other favorite activity—sleeping—is an indication that the turmoil in your life will soon be replaced by tranquility. It may also be trying to tell you that you are in need of a rest.

Speaking Cats

Dreams that involve a cat speaking in a human voice are believed to be highly prophetic in nature. They elevate the cat to the status of divine messenger and need to be carefully analyzed for they often contain an important message from the spirit-dimension, the psychic realm, other worlds, or even divine beings. To interpret such a dream, the words spoken by the cat must be considered. (Keep in mind that their meanings may be obvious, or they may be obscured by arcane symbolism.) Additionally, any other symbols that may appear in the dream should not be overlooked for they can be of equal significance.

Flying Cats

To see a flying or winged cat in your dream indicates a strong connection with the psychic realms. For witches with a cat-familiar, and others who share a closeness with a feline companion, it may actually be an experience indicative of a journey into the astral plane with the cat in its astral form serving as a companion, guide, or protector.

Caged Cat

A caged cat is a dream symbol representing a subconscious feeling of being trapped in an unpleasant situation or perhaps in a boring rut. A caged cat that cries, hisses, or meows loudly is most likely a symbol of you, or a part of yourself (such as your feminine side) that is crying out for liberation.

Bathing a Cat

Bathing a cat could be an indication that a cleansing of the body, mind, or spirit is in order.

Feeding a Cat

Feeding a cat may symbolize a need or desire for spiritual nourishing. Forgetting to feed a cat (or leaving it out in the cold) often indicates that the dreamer is forgetting to care about a part of herself.

Egyptian Cat

An Egyptian cat symbolizes great psychic power and often appears in the dreams of gifted seers, clairvoyants, and those who possess psychic talents that are not yet recognized. To dream that such a cat inspires fear within you may reveal an inner fear of either psychic phenomena in general or your own psychic abilities, determinable by other factors of the actual dream. To be visited in a dream by an Egyptian cat may also signify a spiritual or magickal connection between the dreamer and the ancient Egyptian goddess Bastet—a cat-headed deity whom Herodotus referred to as the "Mistress of the Oracle." (Incidentally, the Egyptian word for cat, *mau,* means "to see.")

Monster Cat

A terrifying monster cat appearing in a dream or in a nightmare can be a symbol of a feared and repressed desire, drive, or emotion, or it may actually be a fearful situation or a painful truth in disguise that is confronting or pursuing you. To dream that you are slaying a monster cat indicates that you are in the process of overcoming your fear; however, to dream that you are trying to escape or hide from the beast

"Minette" (Grandville)

indicates that you are failing to deal with the situation at hand, unable to face your fears, or unwilling to accept the truth. This dream symbol may also represent the loathsome and "monstrous" characteristics of certain individuals who play a key role in your life.

A cat, being the psychic animal that it is, often represents the dreamer's own psychic or intuitive aspects, or it points to a person of a psychic nature who is connected in some way to the dreamer. Sometimes a cat or kitten in a dream actually represents the dreamer and shows the role that he plays in certain situations or in relation to others. Therefore, when attempting to interpret a cat-dream it is important to consider the animal's attitude, emotions, appearance, situation, age, and so on to help focus the message of the dream.

If we pay close attention to our dreams and the symbolic messages they hold, we will be rewarded with a better understanding of our hidden feelings, fears, and desires, and we will be able to make full use of our conscious existence through greater self-awareness and self-healing.

Recommended Dream-Interpretation Books

The Dreamer's Workbook: A Complete Guide to Interpreting and Understanding Dreams by Nerys Dee. New York: Sterling Publishing Company, Inc., 1990.

Gypsy Dream Dictionary by Raymond Buckland. St. Paul, Minn.: Llewellyn Publications. Second Edition, 1999.

The Dream Book: Symbols for Self-Understanding by Betty Richards. Petaluma, Calif.: Inner Light Press, 1983.

The Modern Witch's Dreambook by Sarah Lyddon Morrison. Secaucus, N.J.: Citadel Press, 1990.

4

Felines and Familiars

The familiars of Witches do most ordinarily appear in the shape of Cats, which is an argument that this beast is dangerous to soul and body.

—Perottus

The dawn of the Middle Ages was the beginning of an era shrouded in superstition, sorcery, and the fanatical fear of both God and the Devil. It was also a time when the cat, once worshipped in earlier times as an animal of divine status, found itself in the new role of the witch's familiar.

It was during this period in history that the permanent link between cats and practitioners of the Craft was initially forged. However, the centuries that were dominated by the infamous Inquisition and backdropped by the screams of the tortured and the blood of the innocent were, to put it mildly, not kind to the cat.

The belief in witches (the kind with wart-covered noses, pointed black hats, evil powers, and flying broomsticks) was strong throughout most of Europe during this time. It was also regarded as a fact that most, if not all, witches were assigned by the Devil an imp to serve as a companion and magickal assistant.

Imps, better known as familiars, could appear in any shape or size. However, in order to avoid drawing unwanted attention in a world where witchcraft paranoia and the mere accusation of bewitchment could, and often did, result in arrest, torture, and execution, the familiar wisely took the form of a small ordinary animal such as a toad, a lizard, a raven, a hare, and so forth. Familiars could even manifest themselves as common houseflies, spiders, and other insects if they so desired. However, the most popular type of familiar was the ordinary-looking housecat—especially one with fur as black as pitch.

According to one European legend, cat-familiars preferred to serve female witches, while those that assisted warlocks (a word used in olden times for witches of the male gender) more commonly took the form of a black dog.

Historical Origins

How exactly the association between the cat and the female witch came to be is not known, although some historians suggest that it may be rooted in the ancient Egyptian worship of a major female deity who took the form of a cat. Others believe that the goddess Freya (a Norse and Teutonic deity of love and fertility) was responsible due to the fact that the cat was her sacred animal. When the early Christians, in their conquest of paganism, condemned Freya as a sorceress and heathen goddess of the Devil's employ, the cat instantly became associated with the dark and terrifying world of the occult and the once-forbidden practice of the Black Arts.

Another possible origin of the cat-sorceress connection may be traced back to the ancient Celts who inhabited Gaul (now France) and the British Isles over two thousand years ago. Their priestly caste, the Druids, believed that all cats were actually human beings transformed into animals by the evil powers of

Seventeenth-century woodcut of three witches accompanied by their familiars

sorcery. Just the very sight of a sinister black cat with its yellowish-green eyes glowing eerily in the moonlight was enough to make the blood of even the bravest Druid run as cold as ice.

Each year on October 31 when the Samhain Eve sacrificial bonfires were kindled upon the hilltops, the white-robed priests would round up as many cats and kittens as they could catch, confine them in animal-shaped wickerwork cages, and then cast them into the blaze that illuminated the night sky.

The Druids believed that the purifying powers of fire (especially the sacred flames of Samhain) were the only effective means of destroying a shape-shifting cat-sorceress. To kill such a creature by any other method offered no guarantee that its evil spirit would not return from the dead to forever haunt its executioner or lay a powerful and unbreakable curse upon him and his people.

Another influence was the ancient Roman goddess Diana (also known as the Queen of the Witches) who played a major role in linking the cat to the world of witchcraft. According to mythology, Diana changed places with her brother Lucifer's cat, became impregnated, and then gave birth to a daughter named

Aradia, whom she later sent to earth on a mission to teach witches the secret arts of magick, conjuration, and divination.

Qualities of Familiars

Familiars also possessed shape-shifting abilities and could change their physical shape at will, transforming from one animal into another. Some were unable to be seen by the human eye (except, of course, by the eyes of witches), and in several old witchcraft books there can be found a mention of invisible cat-familiars as well.

According to many writings of the past, it was widely believed in the Middle Ages that all witches who possessed a familiar were obligated by their Satanic pact to feed their faithful imp at least once a day by pricking one of their fingers and allowing the creature to drink a bit of their warm blood. The crimson nectar of fresh human blood not only satisfied the diabolical thirst of the familiar, it was said to be its favorite food.

Familiars were also known to consume human milk at times, or sometimes a combination of human milk and blood. Many lactating witches whose breasts were full with milk would shamelessly allow their familiars to drink from their nipples, according to a number of witch-trial testimonies from both Europe and New England.

An old legend from Scotland and England claims that a witch's familiar was actually a spirit or a low-ranking demon, and fire was the only effective weapon that humans possessed to bring death to one, or (at the very least) to destroy its physical catlike body and deliver the spirit or demonic entity contained within back to the eternal flames of Hell's fiery pit.

Destroying Cats as Devils

Throughout much of Europe in the Dark Ages, untold numbers of innocent cats were believed to be witches' familiars or even witches in disguise, and they were routinely hunted down by the men who made their living as witch-finders. These poor cats often met their death by being burned alive in bonfires, especially on Shrove Tuesday (i.e., the last Tuesday before lent) and Easter—two days of the year when cat-burning rituals took place in great numbers. The feast of Saint John (which falls on June 24) and the first Sunday in Lent were also times when the burning of live cats was common. This barbaric practice not only served to help Christians celebrate their religious feast days, but to drive away all evil forces from the town or village as well.

Under the auspices of the Church, cats would often be suspended over a blazing fire and roasted alive, flayed, or nailed to a cross to simulate the crucifixion of Jesus Christ. They might also be tossed from the belfry of a church, and even placed inside casks and then mercilessly stabbed to death by the sharp swords of bloodthirsty horsemen.

The cries of agonizing pain that issued forth from the tortured and dying cats were said to be "the language of the devils within the body of the Holy Father." The bits and pieces of bones and the ashes that remained after a cat-burning bonfire had concluded would usually be salvaged by the most superstitious of villagers to be used as charms for bringing good luck as well as for keeping the Devil and his unholy demons at bay.

The cat-killing madness continued its sadistic reign for many centuries; and as the feline population reached the point of near extinction, the fate of the cat was beginning to look quite grim. However, a strange twist of fate avenged the cat and eventually put an end to its widespread massacre in the name of Christianity: As the number of cats in Europe became greatly reduced, the rat population was growing to epidemic proportions. This, of course, resulted in the spread of the bubonic plague, known at the time as the Black Death. After it was discovered that rats were to blame for the hellish plague that ravaged Europe and Asia, the senseless killing of the cat finally ceased (despite much protest from the Church), and the cat became highly valued as the human race's only ally against the dreaded disease which, at the time, was without a cure.

(Engraving from *Fox's Book of Martyrs,* sixteenth century)

Infamous Cat-Familiars

A cat-familiar was said to be a gift from the Devil—and a highly valued one at that. In exchange for a bit of milk and blood, it would loyally serve a witch and obey even her most wicked of commands. For this reason, many people in the Middle Ages feared cats just as strongly as they feared witches and the Devil. And for dispatching a "wantoune cat" to work evil deeds on their enemies, many witches—young and old, rich and poor— were sentenced to death.

With the help of their cat-familiars, witches were believed to bring all manner of misfortune upon those who had offended them. One witch was said to have owned a cat-familiar that caused mortal illness simply by blowing its breath upon a child. It also prevented God-fearing Christians from reading their Bibles and was even believed to bring death to the livestock of a farmer who had managed to arouse the witch's anger and hatred.

According to *The Cult of the Cat,* practitioners of sorcery sometimes sacrificed their cat-familiars in order to give power to their curses and spells of black magick. Also, if they found themselves "molested by the Devil," sorcerers often had to resort to sacrificing a live cat. This was said to be the only way to effectively banish the Devil's unholy presence.

In the summer of 1566, three years after Queen Elizabeth's Parliament passed the second of England's three Witchcraft acts, the first notable witch trial to be tested under the new law was held in the town of Chelmsford. The three defendants— Elizabeth Francis, Agnes Waterhouse, and her eighteen-year-old daughter Joan—were accused of bewitching a number of people in their village with the aid of a white-spotted cat by the name of Sathan who supposedly drank human blood, spoke in a human voice, and was able to change itself into both a toad and a black dog. According to the trial records, which are now housed in the Lambeth Palace Library:

First, (Elizabeth Francis) learned this art of Witchcraft at the age of twelve years of her grandmother, whose name (was) Mother Eve of Hatfield Peverell, deceased.

Item: when she taught it to her, she counselled her to renounce God and His word, and to give of her blood to Sathan (as she termed it), which she delivered her in the likeness of a white spotted cat, and taught her to feed the said cat with bread and milk. And she did so. Also she (Mother Eve) taught her to call it by the name of Sathan and to keep it in a basket.

When this Mother Eve had given her the cat Sathan, then this Elizabeth desired first of the said cat that she might be rich and to have goods. And he promised her she should, asking her what she would have. And she said sheep (for this cat spake to her, as she confessed, in a strange hollow voice, but such as she understood by use). And this cat forthwith brought sheep into her pasture to the number of eighteen, black and white, which continued with her for a time, but in the end did all wear away, she knew not how.

Item: when she had gotten these sheep, she desired to have one Andrew Byles to her husband, which was a man of some wealth; and the cat did promise she should, but that he said she must first consent that this Andrew should abuse her, and she so did.

And after, when this Andrew had abused her, he would not marry her. Wherefore she willed Sathan to waste his goods, which he forthwith did. And yet not being contented with this, she willed him to touch his body which he forthwith did, whereof he died.

Item: that every time (Sathan) did anything for her, she said that he required a drop of blood, which she gave him by pricking herself, sometime in one place and then in another; and where she pricked herself remained a red spot, which was still to be seen.

Item: when this Andrew was dead, she doubting (believing) herself with child, willed Sathan to destroy it. And he bade her take a certain herb and drink it, which she did, and destroyed the child forthwith.

Item: when she desired another husband, he promised her another, naming this Francis whom she now hath, but said he is not so rich as the other, willing her to consent unto that Francis in fornication, which she did. And thereof conceived a daughter that was born within a quarter of a year after they were married.

After they were married, they lived not so quietly as she desired, being stirred (as she said) to much unquietness and moved to swearing and cursing. Wherefore she willed Sathan her cat to kill the child, being about the age of half a year old, and he did so. And when she yet found not the quietness she desired, she willed it to lay a lameness in the leg of this Francis, her husband. And it did in this manner: it came in a morning to this Francis' shoe, lying in it like a toad: and when he perceived it, putting on his shoe, and had touched it with his foot, he being suddenly amazed asked of her what it was. And she bade him kill it, and he was forthwith taken with a lameness whereof he cannot be healed.

After all this, when she had kept this cat by the space of fifteen or sixteen years, and as some say (though untruly) being weary of it, she came to one Mother Waterhouse, her neighbor (a poor woman), when she was going to the oven, and desired her to give her a cake, and she would give her a thing that she should be the better for so long as she lived. And this Mother Waterhouse gave her a cake, whereupon she brought her this cat in her apron, and taught her as she was instructed before by her grandmother Eve, telling her that she must call him Sathan, and give him of her blood and bread and milk as before.

Agnes Waterhouse was found guilty of practicing witchcraft and using her sorcery and newly acquired cat-familiar to bring about the deaths of several people as well as neighbors' cattle and geese. She was hanged on July 29, 1566. (According to *The Encyclopedia of Witchcraft and Demonology,* she might have been the first woman to be executed for practicing witchcraft in "modern" England.) Her daughter Joan was found not guilty. Elizabeth Francis, who was found guilty, was sentenced to one year in the jailhouse and four appearances in the pillory. However, three years later she was once again brought before the court in the second mass trial at Chelmsford—this time on charges of using black magick to bring ill health, and ultimately death, to a woman named Alice Poole. She pleaded innocent but was convicted and hanged.

In Windsor, England, a witch trial was held in the year 1579 for a woman who was accused of possessing a spirit in the form of a cat. She confessed that it assisted her in her spell casting, and she nourished it every day with a mixture of milk and some of her own blood. Another witch, who was tried in Essex a few years later, claimed that she was visited nightly by a cat-familiar who would "suckle bloud of her upon her armes and other places of her body." A witch who was tried in Somerset told the court that she often fell into a trancelike state each time her cat-familiar suckled her.

At the St. Osyth witch trials of 1582, an accused witch named Ursula Kempe confessed to having four familiars. One was a gray male cat she called Tittey, and another was a black male cat named Jack. Along with the other familiars, they were fed blood from their witch-mistress's left thigh in exchange for carrying out her *maleficia* (misfortunes, illnesses, and disasters caused by black magick). Jack, the black cat was said to have plagued a neighbor's wife.

In the case of the Warboys witches, a seventy-six-year-old woman named Alice Samuel was said to have caused the death of one prominent Lady Cromwell by making an evil cat-familiar materialize nightly in her dreams and rip apart her flesh with its sharp claws and fangs. These magickally induced nightmares continued for fifteen months, during which time the Lady Cromwell's health declined. In July of 1592 she finally died. Shortly after she was laid to rest, the three young girls of Mrs. Samuel's neighbor, Robert Throckmorton, began experiencing strange and unexplained seizures and accused the old woman of bewitching Lady Cromwell to death. As a result of the children's testimony, Alice Samuel, her husband, and her daughter Agnes were tried in court on April 5, 1593, found guilty, and hanged.

In 1597, what can only be described as a "witch craze" swept over the village of Aberdeen, resulting in twenty-four women and men being burned alive at the stake. One witch, known as Old Janet Wishart, was said to have sent "nightmare cats" to plague her enemies with the most horrible of dreams. These supernatural felines were also her familiars, given to her by the Devil, according to the trial records.

In 1607, a witch trial was held in Edinburgh, Scotland, for Isobel Grierson, the wife of John Bull. Of the six counts against her was one of entering the house of Adam Clark "in likeness of her own cat, accompanied with a great number of other cats, in a devilish manner" and causing what was described as "great and tearful noise and trouble." The cats were believed to be her spirit-familiars, and their evil presence in the house was said to have plagued a servant girl with a mysterious illness that lasted for a period of six weeks.

Margaret and Philippa Flower, the daughters of a reputed witch, had been unpleasantly dismissed from service at the castle of the Earl of Rutland. Out of revenge they turned to their mother's powerful black magick and employed a cat-familiar named Rutterkin to assist them in hexing the Earl's family. After rubbing a stolen glove upon the cat's back and then boiling the glove, pricking it with pins, and burying it in the garden, the Earl's eldest son, Lord Rosse, lost his life. The court found the Flower sisters guilty of causing death by bewitchment, and they were executed at Lincoln, England, in March of 1618.

Elizabeth Clarke, an old woman described as "a one-legged hag," was the first victim of Matthew Hopkins—a ruthless seventeenth-century lawyer who acquired ill fame as England's Witch-Finder General. One of the five familiars Mrs. Clarke confessed to having was a white "kitling" (kitten) named Holt. She was found guilty of "entertaining" evil familiar-spirits and hanged in the year 1645.

Elizabeth Dickenson was one of five witches accused of bewitching an entire English family. At her trial she confessed that her familiar, a cat with fur as white as snow, aided her in all of her magickal workings.

At a witchcraft trial in Sweden in the year 1669, three hundred boys and girls, whose ages ranged from six to sixteen,

Matthew Hopkins, the self-appointed Witch-Finder
General, is pictured here with two witches and their
familiars in animal form. (Frontispiece to Hopkins's
Discovery of Witches, first published in 1647: Rare Book
Division, the New York Public Library)

confessed that they had attended Sabbat meetings and had
signed their names in the Devil's infamous Black Book in exchange for the power to work spells and divine the future.
Each child was said to have received from the Devil at the
time of their initiation into witchcraft "a beast about the big-
ness and shape of a young cat."

In 1673, a witch who belonged to a Northumbrian coven
confessed at a witch trial that she had engaged in a bizarre act.

According to her testimony, another covener had magickally assumed the form of a gray cat that exhaled upon her and put her into a trance. It then placed a bridle upon her and rode her to the Sabbat gathering like a horse. All of this, of course, was said to have been carried out in the Devil's name.

Pyewackett is perhaps the most famous name of all cat-familiars, bringing to mind the witch's cat in the 1958 movie *Bell, Book and Candle*—a romantic comedy about a beautiful young witch (played by Kim Novak) who uses her magickal skills on an unsuspecting publisher (played by James Stewart). However, Pyewackett is actually a cat-familiar name that dates back to Renaissance England, and one which, in the words of Matthew Hopkins, "no mortal could invent."

Witch's Butter

According to old Swedish folklore, a strange substance known as "witch's butter" was actually the vomit of cats belonging to witches. It was said to have been yellow in color and was often found in gardens.

Hundreds of years ago, many people in Sweden believed that witches sent their loyal cat-familiars out at night to steal food from their neighbors' gardens and unlocked kitchens. The cats, possessing such ravenous appetites, often consumed so much of the stolen food that it caused them to regurgitate on the spot. Their vomit was believed to be extremely poisonous, and it was sometimes used by witches as an ingredient of cauldron brews concocted for bringing severe illness or death to an enemy.

Modern Witches and Their Familiars

The relationship between the witch and the familiar continues on into the present day and has definitely come a long way since the Middle Ages. The cat-familiars of contemporary witches, Wiccans, and pagans are far from being the demonic imps that they were portrayed to be in olden times. Their purpose is not to perform evil deeds. They do not drink the blood and milk of their human counterparts in exchange for their supernatural services, and they are neither born in the fires of Hell nor given to a witch by the Prince of Darkness in exchange for her soul. Rather, they are a witch's animal friend, faithful companion, coven mascot, and magickal inspiration. To some witches they are even regarded as a member of the family or believed to be the reincarnation of a past-life relative, friend, or lover.

Luckily cats are no longer burned alive for being demons in disguise, and witches are no longer executed for being "in league with the Devil," which is a practice that modern day witches are not guilty of in any manner. (The Devil is an entity that is connected mainly to the Christian faith and not to the modern witchcraft movement that is based largely in part upon the shamanistic and Goddess-oriented earth and fertility religions that once flourished throughout pre-Christian Europe, Ireland, and Great Britain.)

The term *familiar* is sometimes used to describe any pet owned by a witch. But the truth of the matter is that witches and their familiars have a special connection that extends beyond what is regarded as the average owner-and-pet relationship. They share between them what can be described as a loving, spiritual, magickal, and psychic bond. It is said that such a bond remains strong in the afterlife and may even transcend different incarnations.

Not every modern witch owns a cat, but I am confident that the ones who do will agree that their furry, purring friends are magickal in their own right. They may not possess the supernatural power to literally shape-shift or master invisibility, but without a doubt they are graceful creatures, loyal and loving, with a mystique that is uniquely their own.

The cat shall always be regarded as the most popular familiar of those who follow the path of the Old Religion. And beautiful indeed is the sight of a cat with eyes alive with magick and mystery, gracing us with their presence as we witches cast our circles and perform our rites to honor the gods of old and to celebrate the changing of the seasons.

Naming Your Familiar

Choosing the right name for your familiar is often not an easy task. Once you decide on a name and your cat becomes accustomed to the sound of his name, it will be next to impossible to change it later and expect the animal to respond to its new name. Cats, like many people, are not partial to change.

It is not uncommon for many witches' familiars (and even their children) to be named after pagan gods and goddesses, mythological beings, magickal herbs, gemstones, characters from fantasy or science fiction literature, and things associated with Mother Nature.

How do you know when you've found the right name? Usually you will just know as soon as you hear it. Its "vibrations" will just feel right and you may even experience a warm tingling sensation throughout your body.

Many witches and other magickally minded individuals receive names through spirit channeling, meditative rituals, dreams, and various methods of divination, such as pendulum dowsing and Ouija board consultation.

Once you have decided upon a name for your familiar, speak it out loud several times as you stroke your familiar's fur and ask the cat if she likes the name you've chosen. If the cat purrs and offers a positive response, you have a winner. However, if the cat growls, hisses, scratches, walks away from you, swishes its tail angrily from side to side, or behaves in any negative manner, it is probably a good idea to come up with another name. Eventually you and your familiar will find a name that you can both agree upon.

Names should always be chosen with care, keeping in mind the meaning (and power) behind a name, as well as any numerological significance it may possess.

The following section contains many magickal names that are ideal for cats (and other types of familiars as well). In many instances, the source of these names and their meanings are included. A few of the names are ones that I personally have used for my own cats. Some of the names are exotic and uncommon, and some are popular among cat-lovers of the Wiccan and Neo-Pagan communities. Hopefully this list will provide you with the right name you've been searching for, or inspire you to come up with one of your own.

Abracadabra   An ancient magickal charm.

Aladdin   Master of a secret cave of treasures, from *Arabian Nights.*

Alakazam   A famous "magic word" popularly used by stage magicians.

Alchemy   The ancient art of transmutation.

Atlantis   A legendary sunken continent whose inhabitants were known for their telepathic powers and use of crystals.

Avalon   The otherworld of Celtic mythology and Arthurian lore.

Ayesha   An African word meaning "sorceress."

Balisarda   A legendary sword of magick.

Banshee   In Gaelic folklore, a wailing spirit that presages death.

Bast, Bastet   Ancient Egyptian cat-goddess.

Befana   An Italian word meaning "good fairy."

Belladonna   A poisonous plant associated with witches and magick.

Brew   A witch's magickal concoction.

Brimstone   An archaic word for sulfur.

Broosha   In the folklore of Spanish Jews, Lilith (the first wife of Adam) in the form of a huge, blood-drinking, black cat.

Cabala, Kabbalah   A medieval system of Jewish mysticism.

Camelot   The legendary kingdom of King Arthur.

Casmira   A mystic from Voltaire's *Candide.*

Cassandra   A Trojan prophetess called Daughter of Hecate.

Catnip   An aromatic herb intoxicating to, and beloved by, most cats. It is sacred to Bast and is used by many witches for cat-magick.

Cattywampas   A hobgoblin.

Charmer   One who uses charms, magickal and otherwise.

Circe   The beautiful enchantress from Homer's *The Odyssey.*

Cloot, Clootie   Scottish nickname for the Devil.

Cobweb   The name of a fairy from William Shakespeare's *A Midsummer Night's Dream.* An ideal name for a fluffy gray cat.

Crystal   An amuletic or talismanic piece of quartz.

Damian   A traditional male witch name (from Greek *daimon,* "a spirit").

Darkshadow   A dark gray or black cat might like this name.

Diablo   The Spanish word for *devil.* A good name for a mischievous cat or one possessing a wicked temper.

Diva   A Latin word meaning "goddess."

Draco   A dragon.

Elf-Chaser   A good name for a cat who plays with the fairy-folk.

Elvina   A name meaning "befriended by the elves."

Elvira   Mistress of the Dark.

Enchantra   An enchanting name.

Endora   Samantha Stevens's mother on the television show, *Bewitched;* a name inspired by the Witch of Endor, who (according to the Old Testament) foretold men's fortunes by the inspiration of a conjured spirit.

Equinox   The time when day and night are equal.

Esmeralda   The Gypsy woman from *The Hunchback of Notre Dame.*

Ethereal   Celestial or delicate.

Excalibur   King Arthur's magickal sword.

Fantasia   Another word for fantasy.

Fata Morgana   A medieval term for illusions or mirages.

Fay   An elf or fairy.

Galinthias   A servant women who was changed into a cat by the goddess Hera.

Gandalf   Tolkien's wizard.

Genie   A supernatural being that grants three wishes.

Ghost   An ideal name for a pale-colored cat.

Gloriana   A fairy from Spenser's *Faerie Queene.*

Griezzell Greedigutt   An unusual familiar's name mentioned in *Discovery of Witches* by Matthew Hopkins, Witch-Finder General, 1647.

Grimalkin   An old cat, especially a she-cat; a familiar name popular in the Middle Ages and used mainly for gray cats.

Grizelda   A traditional witch name.

Gypsy   Ideal for a cat that likes to wander.

Hemlock   A poisonous plant associated with witchcraft.

Hex, Hex-Cat, Hexter   Any name with *hex* in it is a good name for a witch's cat, especially if it is a black one. *Hex* is the German word for "witch."

Hobgoblin   A mischievous elf.

Houdini   A famous stage magician.

Jack   The name of a black cat familiar belonging to Ursula Kempe, who was hanged as a witch in St. Osyth, England, in 1582.

Jinx   A person or thing that supposedly brings bad luck.

Juju   A powerful African charm.

Kismet   An Arabic word meaning "fate" or "destiny."

Kundalini   A Sanskrit word meaning "serpent power."

Lightfoot   The name of a sixteenth-century witch's cat-familiar from Essex, England.

Lorelei   In mythology, a beautiful siren who lures men with songs.

Magico   An Italian word meaning "magick."

Malagigi   An Italian word meaning "magician."

Manda   A Hindu name meaning "lord of the occult."

Mandala   A sacred diagram or meditation symbol.

Mandragora   Another name for a mandrake.

Mandrake   The most magickal of all plants.

Mephistopheles   A famous demon to whom Faust sold his soul.

Merlin   The most famous wizard of all time.

Midnight   Twelve o'clock at night has long been regarded as the witching hour—a time of great magickal and supernatural power, when many spells traditionally are cast and when the restless spirits of the dead rise up from their graves.

Moonshadow An appropriate name for a cat born during the waning or dark phase of the moon, or during a lunar eclipse.

Morgan le Fay Queen of the Shades.

Noggles A race of mischievous gray-colored fairies from western Europe, who are said to dwell in the country near sylvan streams.

Nostradamus A famous sixteenth-century French seer.

Oberon The king of the fairies, from *A Midsummer Night's Dream*.

Obsidian A glassy volcanic rock said to protect against negativity.

Omen A sign of things to come.

Onyx A good name for a black cat.

Orenda An Iroquois word meaning "magickal power."

Orion Lord of the Hunt.

Orrthannan A Gaelic word meaning "enchantment."

Ouija A special board used for communication with spirits.

Pandora A good name for a cat who likes to open up doors, poke her nose into everything, and get into mischief. Cats named Pandora usually do not take stock in the old saying "Curiosity killed the cat."

Panpipes A musical instrument associated with the Horned God.

Pawpaw A tree with purple flowers and yellow fruit.

Phantom Another word for a ghost.

Pharaoh A title bestowed upon the kings of ancient Egypt. A perfect name for any regal cat or one accustomed to being treated like a king.

Pillywiggin According to Welsh and English folklore, a race of winged pixielike creatures that live and play among the springtime wildflowers. A cute name for a cute cat.

Pixie, Pixy In Scottish folklore, a capricious and often mischievous type of fairy said to be partial to flowers.

Pooka An Irish fairy.

Pyewackett A traditional witch's familiar name, and also the name of the cat from John Van Druten's *Bell, Book and Candle*.

Rasputin Famous Russian occultist and court magician.

Raven   A black bird with occult association.

Rowan   A tree associated with witches.

Runes   Ancient Norse and Teutonic alphabet sigils used in some rituals of magick and divination.

Sabrina   A traditional witch name.

Sage   A wise man or wizard; also an herb associated with smudging.

Salem   A Massachusetts city infamous for witch trials in 1692. Ironically, the name "Salem" derives from the Hebrew word *shalom,* which means "peace."

Samantha   The nose-twitching witch who was married to "a mortal" on TV's *Bewitched.* A popular name for Siamese cats.

Samhain   Another name for Halloween, an important witches' Sabbat.

Sathan   The infamous cat-familiar of Mother Agnes Waterhouse.

Shadow   Another word for a ghost; also, to follow and watch closely.

Shalimar   A mystical garden of love.

Shaman   One who practices the magickal, spiritual system of shamanism.

Shambhala   A legendary Tibetan kingdom of spiritual enlightenment.

Shazam   Famous "magic words" used by stage magicians.

Sheba (or *Shayba*)   The Arabic-Aramaean name for the Great Goddess whose spirit dwelt within a sacred black stone at Mecca.

Sibyl   A woman with prophetic power.

Spell-binder, Spell-caster   One who casts spells.

Sphinx   An Egyptian statue of a recumbent lion with a man's head; also a mythological winged lion with a woman's head.

Spook, Spooky   An ideal name to give a scary-looking cat or one that is easily spooked.

Stargazer   Another name for an astrologer.

Tabitha   A traditional name for a witch's tabby cat. It means "graceful" and was also the name of TV witch Samantha Stevens's daughter.

Taboo   A system among natives of the Pacific islands by which certain persons and objects are set aside as sacred or accursed; anything that is forbidden.

Tarot   A special deck of cards used for divination.

Tempest   A violent wind storm.

Titania   Queen of the fairies, from *A Midsummer Night's Dream.*

Vamp   An adventuress or seductress.

Vinegar Tom   A famous cat-familiar from the Middle Ages. An ideal name for a witch's tomcat.

Voodoo   A religious, magickal system based on ancient African rites and Catholicism.

Warlock   A name once used for a male witch.

Willow   A tree associated with witchcraft and divination.

Witch Hazel   A good name for a green-eyed cat.

Recommended Reading

Cat Calls by Alastair MacGregor. New York: E.P. Dutton, 1988. Cat names through the ages, historical, literary, for every breed and personality.

The Cat Name Companion: Facts and Fables to Help You Name Your Feline by Mark Bryant. Secaucus, N.J.: Citadel Press, 1995. This is an excellent book to consult when you are searching for the perfect name for your cat. Over 2,000 names, each with its derivation and explanation, are presented. The names of numerous pagan gods and goddesses are mentioned throughout, and many names suitable for a witch's familiar can be found. Additionally, this book lists enough cat anecdotes to please even the most finicky of ailurophiles.

The Complete Book of Magical Names by Phoenix McFarland. St. Paul, Minn.: Llewellyn Publications, 1996. Written by a Wiccan priestess, this book contains close to 5,000 nonbiblical names and their meanings. It is an ideal resource for choosing "witchy" and out of the ordinary cat names, as well as unique names for babies, magickal names for witches, and even coven names.

What to Name the Cat by Thelma Kandel. New York: Linden Press, 1983. This 160-page paperback book covers thousands of cute, exotic, and unusual names for cats, including many that are of an astrological, magickal, and mythological nature.

A Cat-Naming Ritual

The following ritual can be performed when naming a new cat or when giving a magickal name to a familiar. It can also be utilized as a wiccaning or paganing ceremony for newborn kittens. (Wiccanings and paganings are similar in many ways to baptisms and are generally performed by a High Priestess or High Priest of the Craft when a newborn child of a Wiccan or pagan couple is ritually presented with a magickal or nonmagickal name.)

When the Moon is new (which is the traditional time for performing rituals and spell-work connected with beginnings and new things), cast a magick circle in a clockwise manner and summon the elemental spirits of Air, Fire, Water, and Earth.

In the center of the circle, either upon an altar or the floor, light a brand new cat-shaped candle that has been anointed with a few drops of catnip essential oil or any oil that magickally corresponds to the cat's astrological sign (if known).

Take the cat lovingly in your arms. Gently stroke the animal's fur, and when it begins to purr, visualize the cat surrounded by a protective aura of white light and then recite nine times the following pagan prayer (once for each of the cat's nine lives):

> [Name] is the name I give to thee.
> [Name] is the one who ye shall be.
> And may the sound of thy new name
> Magick and power ninefold claim.
> May ye live free and blessed be
> By goddess Bastet. So mote it be!

Beltane kittens at a wiccaning ceremony. It was once believed that "May kittlings" (kittens born in the month of May) were extremely unlucky and should not be allowed to live. (Photo by Gerina Dunwich)

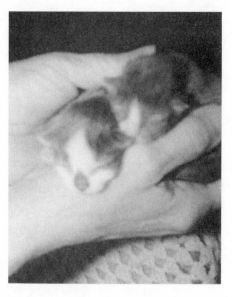

After the prayer has been recited, take a consecrated athame (ritual dagger) or wand and use it to trace the sacred symbol of the pentacle in the air over the cat. Give the cat a kiss; then give thanks and bid farewell to the elemental spirits. Uncast the circle in a counterclockwise manner, and extinguish the candle. The cat-naming ritual is now complete.

A Blessing for Familiars

When the midnight hour is bathed in the soft glow of the moon at her fullest, cast a magick circle in a clockwise fashion and within it light a new and properly anointed cat-shaped candle.

Place a small or medium-size cast-iron cauldron next to the candle and upon a heat-proof stand. (If your cauldron does not have a stand, you can use a brick or a wooden cutting board.) Pour about one-half of a cup of rubbing alcohol into the cauldron and then carefully toss in a lit match. As the flames of the cauldron dance and fill the circle with light, warmth, and magick, hold the cat in your arms and recite the following poetic blessing:

> O cat-familiar,
> Companion and friend,

To thee a witch's blessing I send
By rhyme of enchantment
And love's potent power,
By candle anointed
And magickal hour,
By Moon's silver charm
And night's dark desire,
By elements ancient
And cauldron of fire.

Be blessed by the Goddess
And Horned One so old,
Be blessed by the forces
Of nature so bold,
By wind and by water,
By earth and by flame,
By every deity's unspoken name.

Blessings abundant
Be now upon thee.
Harming none, this is done.
So mote it be!

Allow the fire in the cauldron to burn itself out, which should happen within a matter of minutes. Warning: Do not touch any part of the cauldron with your bare hands because the cast iron will be extremely hot and you may receive a serious burn if you are not careful! Be sure to use heat-resistant pot holders or oven mitts to protect your hands if you must come into contact with the cauldron before it cools completely.

Extinguish the cat-candle and then uncast the circle in a counterclockwise fashion. (Please note: Should you feel it necessary to make any changes or additions to this, or any other,

Quicksilver waits upon a snow-covered stone altar in the woods for the coven to gather for a Full Moon Ritual. (Photo by Gerina Dunwich)

ritual, please feel free to do so. The more you personalize your magickal craft, the better the results shall be for you. And always remember that the words you recite in an incantation, prayer, or chant are not nearly as important as the intent behind them.)

5

The Totem Cat

The totem, which is traditionally associated with shamanistic paths and Native American spirituality, is a person's spiritual guardian or a clan's guiding spirit that usually manifests itself in the form of an ordinary animal of the wild.

According to some Native American traditions (especially of the Pacific coast tribes), guardian spirits roamed the earth in animal form to assist humans in various ways—from teaching magick, to giving strength and courage, to helping one develop a specialized skill. Totems also taught prayers, sacred songs, and secret dances. They could even make themselves invisible and enter a human being's soul. Some animal totems represented a clan or the branches of a family tree, and their images were often carved on columns of wood known as totem poles.

The word *totem* derived from the Ojibwa term *odem,* which means "the mystic bond between the spirit, the place, and the people."

Totems and Familiars

The totem and the traditional witch's familiar share a few similarities. They both may appear in the form of a cat or other animal; and both can be called upon through meditation quests, spell-work, and various other methods.

It is said that in some cases a witch's familiar may also serve as her or his personal totem; however, not all totems are familiars. In fact, totems and familiars are two entirely different entities. The main function of the witch's familiar is the role of magickal assistant and companion, but those of the totem include teacher, power spirit, and protector. The totem can also serve as a symbol of one's true nature or of the particular aspects one needs to incorporate into his life. It is in these ways that a totem can be beneficial to an individual on a quest for spiritual enlightenment and fulfillment.

In most cases a witch's familiar takes the form of a living animal (or in certain instances a supernatural, animal-like creature). But a totem does not necessarily have to be an animal. Creatures of the wild (such as bears, wolves, coyotes, and birds) are the most common forms of totems; however, totems can take the form of many things from a tree to an insect to even a creature from the mythical realms—such as a dragon, unicorn, phoenix, and so forth. Also, any gift from Mother Nature can serve as a totem. These can include such things as crystals and gemstones, seashells, flowers, fossils, and so on. However, since the theme of this book is cats, this chapter will focus solely on the cat as a totem animal, what a totem cat represents, and how to recognize or make contact with one.

The Cat as a Power Animal

The cat is an animal that symbolizes many positive attributes. Among these are: balance, confidence, courage, independence, recuperative power, second sight, swiftness, and wisdom. The cat has also been associated with the practice of magick since times most olden. As a totem (or power animal) the cat represents a spirit guide who possesses great strength and is both resourceful and brave.

Individuals whose totem animal is the cat are often independent in their lifestyles, and greatly influenced by the creative energies that are conjured when the dark shadows of night and silver moonlight rays dance together.

When a totem cat makes its presence known to you, you may find yourself experiencing an increase in your spiritual energy, physical and mental agility, vision, hunting skills, and self-confidence. If there are certain individuals in your life who have been using intimidation to manipulate you, your feline spirit helper will stand by your side and teach you how to keep yourself from being further victimized in such a manner.

Often a totem cat will come into your life at a time when you are experiencing, or about to experience, a great imbalance of energies. As your guide, it may reveal to you the cause of the imbalance, as well as the steps you must take in order for balance to be restored.

When you embark on a spirit journey with a cat totem, you should always expect the unexpected. The unknown is waiting to be explored, and this applies not only to the physical world around you, but to outer worlds and inner worlds as well. One must take care, however, not to be tempted by, or become addicted in any way to the darker side of the occult. Not only can it be potentially dangerous, it can lead you astray from your spiritual path to enlightenment.

Many contemporary pagans and Wiccans, who either practice shamanism or incorporate elements of it into their ritual-work, feel connected with the cat as a totem animal on a meditative, magickal, or spiritual level. The cat, with its age-old association with witchcraft and its abundance of mystical charm, seems a natural totem animal for witches and all folks who live a magickal lifestyle.

A Russian peasant sketch from the late
nineteenth century

This is not to say that a witch or other individual whose
totem animal is the cat cannot have other animal totems in addition. As a matter of fact, most people do have more than one
totem. Just as two teachers teach their students important
lessons in different subjects and different ways, so do totems. For
instance, a bear totem may indicate strength, a dog totem may
indicate loyalty, a bird totem may indicate freedom or the need
for grounding, and so forth.

It is interesting to note that many American Indian tribes,
including the Pueblo, have associated the cat with witches
since the animal was first brought to the new world by the
European settlers. Undoubtedly, the cat's eerie glowing eyes,
spark-emitting fur, and nocturnal prowling habits helped to link

it to the world of the witch's craft, as well as to the Devil and
the dark, mysterious forces of the occult.

For information on additional animal totems, the following
book is recommended as an excellent resource: *Totems: The
Transformative Power of Your Personal Animal Totem* by Brad
Steiger; New York: Harper Collins Publishers, 1997.

Recognizing Your Totem

At this point you are probably wondering how it is possible to
distinguish your totem animal from any other ordinary animal
you may encounter. A clue can often be found in the way the
animal is behaving, especially if it seems out of the ordinary. For
instance, a wild bird that lands on your shoulder, a deer that
comes up to you without fear as though it has known you since
birth, or a strange animal that appears seemingly out of nowhere to warn you of an impending danger could very well be
your totem animal—especially if you find yourself experiencing
repeated encounters with the same animal.

Totem animals will sometimes display an unusual character-
istic, such as a strangeness or glowing light in their eyes, a brilliant
aura, the power of human speech (either verbally or telepathically), the ability to shape-shift, and so forth. Or you may recognize your totem animal simply by an instinctive feeling or
clairvoyant impression.

A totem animal may be encountered in many places—on a
forest path, in a medicine wheel or magickal circle, on top of
a sacred mountain, in the middle of the city, or even in your
own backyard garden—just to name a few. They have also been
known to appear in dreams, trance states, astral projections, and
near-death experiences when the spirit has left the physical
body. Totems can also manifest at any time during the day or
the night.

The message that the totem holds for you may be an obvious
one, or it may be in the form of a symbolic riddle, depending

upon the situation. Quite often the steps you must take and the things you need to experience in order to discover the true meaning of the message are, in themselves, vital parts of your lesson in life.

Totem Dream Spell

To invite a cat totem to visit you in your dreams, perform the following dream spell before you go to bed.

Anoint a new white candle with three drops of catnip essential oil. (If you are unable to obtain catnip essential oil, you may use three drops of heliotrope or lavender essential oil in place of it.) Light the candle, and then light a charcoal block until it glows, and place it in a fireproof incense burner. Sprinkle a pinch of dried catnip over the charcoal block and then close your eyes and clear your mind of all distracting thoughts, concentrating only upon the image of a cat in your mind's eye. When you feel that the time is right, begin speaking to the cat totem, either verbally or telepathically, and invite it to come to you in your dreams.

If you are insincere, skeptical, or fearful, it is doubtful that your totem will make its presence known to you. You cannot hide your true feelings from an entity of the spirit realm. It will know whether your intentions are true or false.

After requesting the presence and guidance of your totem, be sure to give plenty of thanks. Extinguish the candle, using a snuffer or by pinching out the flame with your moistened fingertips, and then go to sleep. When you awaken, be sure to immediately write down your dream before it fades from your memory as the morning light fills your eyes.

If any type of feline (including the big cats such as lions, panthers, pumas, leopards, or tigers) appeared in your dream or nightmare, the chances are quite good that you have successfully made contact with your cat totem. Be sure to pay special attention to all details of the dream, no matter how insignificant they may seem. Also record and interpret any and all symbols, regardless of how confusing or meaningless they may first appear to be. Symbols are the true language of our dreams, and often a totem's message can be found within them after they are decoded and pieced together like a jigsaw puzzle.

If your dream contained animals other than a cat, it means that you are meant to experience these different animal totems while on the present path of your spiritual journey. There is a reason behind everything. This does not mean that you will never encounter a cat totem at a future time. For all you know, you may have already connected with one in the past without even being aware of it.

Do not become discouraged if you are unsuccessful at first in trying to contact your totem. It may take a few tries, or maybe even more. If you still have no luck after a number of attempts, then you should accept the fact that you are not ready for the experience, for whatever reason. But when the time is finally right and you are ready and willing with an open heart and an open mind, your totem will come. Perhaps not in a dream or a vision, but in another way.

> *The cat is for those who care for the*
> *subtle intimacies of the spirit.*
>
> —Frank Swinnerton

6

Cat Omens
and Superstitions

Beware of people who dislike cats.
—Irish saying

The cat is an animal surrounded by a world of mystery and enchantments, both wicked and wondrous. It is hardly surprising that the cat has inspired more superstitions and omens than any other living thing on earth (with perhaps the exception of humans). Since the dawn of time the cat has been regarded as the harbinger of both good and evil. Diviners have praised this animal as everything from a feline forecaster of weather to the purring prognosticator of love and matrimony.

Many of the old myths and legends surrounding the cat have been claimed by the dark shadows of the distant past, living on only in dust-covered volumes on library shelves and in the bits and pieces of lore handed down from one generation to the next. However, a large number of ancient signs and superstitious beliefs have survived to the present day.

Nine Lives

One of the oldest, as well as most widespread, of all cat superstitions that refuses to fade away into the realm of the forgotten is the one that endows all cats with nine lives. In the worlds of religion and the occult, nine is a very lucky and highly mystical number (the product of three—the sacred number of the Trinity and the Triple Goddess—multiplied by three), and it is probable that the nine-lives myth originated in ancient Egypt where the cat was bestowed with divine status. (The Egyptian pantheon was made up of three companies of nine deities, and nine was therefore regarded as a number of the highest expression of honor.)

It has been said that women and witches, like cats, also possess nine lives, and that nine years of extremely bad luck befalls

Illustration from *The Historie of Four-Footed Beasties* by Edward Topsell, 1658 (The New York Public Library Picture Collection)

any individual who dares to take the life of a cat—one jinxed year for each of the cat's nine lives.

Cats' Eyes

According to Plutarch (an early Greek author who influenced philosophers and writers for centuries), the eyes of all cats wax (enlarge) when the moon is waxing, and wane (contract) when the moon is waning. This myth is connected to the old belief that cats can see in the dark.

In the Middle Ages, it was a popular belief among witch-hunters that the shining of a cat's eyes at night was produced by the flames burning in the fiery pit of Hell.

All cats are born with the natural ability to see auras, ghosts, fairies, and all supernatural entities that are normally invisible to the naked human eye.

Cutting a cat's whiskers is said to impair the cat's vision or even render it temporarily sightless. While it is a fact that a cat's whiskers function in a way similar to a sensory organ, there is no truth whatsoever in the whisker-cutting superstition.

If you desire to see the spirit-world or the enchanted and invisible realm of the fairy-folk, all you need to do is look into the eyes of a cat, according to an old Celtic superstition. The Celts believed that cats' eyes were actually the windows of the fairy king's abode. A brave soul could peek in and witness an inner world, while the fairies were able to peek out from the other side and see the world of mortals.

Cats, Children, and Babies

Cats have long been accused of suffocating children, as well as invalids and the elderly, as they sleep by perching on their chests and sucking out their breath in a manner similar to a vampire sucking out a human being's life blood. It is amazing that a good portion of the population continues to put stock in this age-old, erroneous myth!

If a child and a kitten are delivered into the world on the same day, some say that one will thrive and the other will not. In a similar version of this superstitious belief, the child will suffer ill health or not grow unless the kitten is found a new home at once. It is bad luck to rear babies and kittens together.

It is an old Russian folk-belief that if a cat is placed in the cradle of a newborn baby, it will prevent evil ghosts from possessing the soul of, or doing harm to, the child. Cats have long been valued in the former Soviet Union for having the power to drive away all evil entities of supernatural origin.

A very old, and quite bizarre, superstition from Scotland claims that if a woman unknowingly consumes food that a male cat has ejaculated upon, she will soon find herself pregnant with kittens! The only way to remedy this condition was for the impregnated woman to drink a specially prepared magickal potion, no doubt consisting of ingredients equally as weird as the purpose for which they were intended.

Fertility

The cat is an animal that excels in fecundity, which is why many farmers in Europe once believed that the burying of a live cat in a field was the key to producing a bountiful crop. Upon death, the cat's spirit would become as one with the soil, enriching the land with the cat's magickal powers of abundant fertility.

The Harbinger of Death

In Germany, a number of old beliefs pertain to the cat as a harbinger of death: If a black cat jumps onto the bed where a sickly person lies, this is taken as a sure sign that the person will soon meet with the Grim Reaper. Also, if an old or very ill person witnesses two cats engaged in combat, it is said to be his death omen. This legend further states that the two cats are actually the Devil and an angel in disguise, and that they are fighting over the soul of the person soon to die.

An ancient Chinese belief was that a dead person could return to the world of the living in the form of a cat in order to seek revenge against his or her enemies.

Another Oriental folk-belief held that if a person had a fear of cats (a condition known as ailurophobia), this was an indication that he or she was a rat in a previous life!

Superstitious Christians once believed that when a cat was seen walking over someone's grave, it meant that the Devil had claimed that person's soul.

Luck: Good and Bad

In the United States, Ireland, and other parts of the world, black cats have long been regarded by many superstitious individuals as the bringers of bad luck, especially if they cross your path. (To prevent the black cat from bringing you misfortune, occult tradition holds that you must immediately change your course, cross your fingers, or spit upon the ground.) The Normandy version of this superstition claims that a person's death within the year is portended by a cat of black color crossing her path in the light of the moon. The black cat is an omen of both poverty and ill health in the country of China, but a symbol of good fortune elsewhere in the Orient.

The old superstition surrounding the unlucky black cat made for a rather offbeat article in the November 11, 1942, edition of the *New York Times*. It read: "All black cats in this municipality (French Lick Springs, Indiana) will wear bells on Friday the 13th, by municipal decree, as a war measure to alleviate mental strain on the populace. The practice was introduced on Friday, October 13, 1939, and enforced on all fateful Fridays since, except last year, when a number of minor mishaps occurred."

The black cat is a good-luck animal in England and Scotland (but only if it is entirely black). If you make a sincere wish when one crosses your path, legend has it that your wish will be granted. However, if a black cat begins to cross your path and then turns back, if it is observed from behind, or if it sits with its back to you, the omen connected to these events is not said to be one of good luck.

White and gray cats are believed to be the bringers of good luck in the United States, Belgium, and Spain. But in Scotland and Ireland the most auspicious of all cats is the one that possesses three colors. All homes with a three-colored cat (also known as a calico) are said to be protected against harm. Orange or tabby cats were once believed to bring good luck in abundance, but only to witches. Cats with double claws are also prized as lucky omens and charms.

In ancient times it was not uncommon for cats to be sealed alive into the walls of houses, convents, and public buildings. This cruel practice was done to ensure good luck and guard against catastrophes, such as fires and natural disasters.

Many actors and others involved in the theater believe that it is bad luck for a cat to run across the stage while a play is being acted out. Apart from stealing the show (as cats seem to have a way of doing), the presence of a cat on a stage or anywhere within a theater has been blamed for fires, power outages, accidents, injuries, and even a play's bad review or premature closing.

European legend holds that stray tortoiseshell-colored cats carry with them bad luck and should never, under any circumstances, be allowed into the home. Additionally, white cats cannot be trusted, and if one should cross your path, you must cross your fingers to avoid bad luck. The act of spitting in the presence of a white cat is also supposed to avert misfortune.

It is good luck to allow a stray black cat into your home if it wishes to enter, but bad luck to drive it away. In Oxford there is an old wives' tale that warns of inviting Death to visit your family by driving a black cat away from your house.

A belief popular among many seafaring men in the Middle Ages was that bad luck fell on anyone who tossed a cat overboard or drowned it at sea. To do so was also believed to create storms. (See also the section on Weather Prognostications, page 99.)

Good luck is indicated by the sneezing of a cat; however, if a cat sneezes three times, all members of the family will soon catch a cold.

In England it is said to be most unlucky for anyone to keep alive a "May Kittling" (a cat born on any day in the month of May). In addition to being the bringers of ill luck, they are believed to be ineffective mouse-catchers that frequently take pleasure in bringing snakes and worms into the house. Many even possess a strange penchant for suffocating infants. Not only are May-born cats believed unlucky, all cats and kittens that are given or received as gifts any time during the month of May are equally as ominous.

An old superstition among many miners is that it is extremely bad luck to see a cat (or to even say the word "cat") while in a mine. To do so has been said to result in freak accidents, injuries, cave-ins, and even the loss of life. Supposedly, the only way to break the jinx is to kill the cat that is seen.

In nineteenth-century Great Britain, many fishermen dared not say aloud the word *cat* for they, too, believed that the very sound of this "taboo word" brought bad luck and disaster. Instead, they would refer to a cat as a *fitting, foodin, kirser,* or *vengla.*

Bad luck is said to soon find its way into the lives of those whose cats jump on a table, according to an old superstitious belief that hails from Somerset, England. (Anyone who has ever had a cat jump upon a table and knock over a delicate, expensive figurine or ruin the main course of a holiday dinner will surely attest to this!)

In some parts of the world it was believed that to deliberately kill a cat was to invite Death into your home or to sacrifice your soul to the Devil. Some people even believed that if you killed a cat, its angry ghost would avenge the killing by taking possession of you. If a farmer was foolish enough to drown a cat or a kitten, his livestock would soon succumb to sickness and possibly death.

However, one does not necessarily have to kill a cat in order to suffer bad luck. To merely kick a cat is enough to cause rheumatism to develop in your legs, and of course any harm that you may bring upon a cat will be returned threefold to you by the law of karma.

Memory Loss

It was once forbidden for Jewish boys in Russia to pet any cat for it was believed that if a boy stroked the fur of a cat, his memory would vanish. Whether it was a temporary or permanent memory loss is not known, nor is the reason behind this peculiar superstitious belief.

Money-Magnet Cats

It is said that a cat with a "smutty nose" possesses the power to attract money to its mistress or master like a magnet. If you wash the soot off of a cat's nose, you will wash away all of your future prosperity. A white cat, with or without a "smutty nose," will bring you money if you spit upon the ground as soon as it crosses your path.

There exists an old Japanese legend that says if you treat a cat well and share your food with it without any thought of gain, the cat will reward you with riches and all that you desire. This superstitious belief is reflected within the themes of many childrens' fairy tales from olden times.

The Mouser

If money is used to purchase a cat, this is believed by some to jinx the mouse-catching abilities of the animal. The best mousers are always the cats and kittens that are received as gifts.

The old expression, "A cat that's bought is good for naught" is still taken as gospel in many parts of the world.

Mantic Arts, Romantic Hearts

If you are a single woman or man and happen to be the first person a cat looks at after it has licked itself clean, this is said to be an indication that you will marry at a young age.

In Scotland it was once believed that if a young lady kept a black cat in the house as a pet, she would never be without gentlemen callers. However, if she kept more than one male cat, it would bring her more than one marriage.

If the sneezing of a cat is witnessed by a bride on her wedding day, this is thought to be a very good omen. It is said to portend a marriage blessed with love, happiness, and fidelity. The giving of a cat as a wedding gift also ensures a happy and prosperous married life for the newlywed couple.

Wedding bells will soon ring for a member of the family if a strange white cat comes to the house and suns itself on the doorstep. However, in the United States, if a black cat is seen on the doorstep of a woman or man on the morning of their wedding day, this is believed to be quite an ill omen. Heed the warning of the black cat and either postpone the wedding at once or call it off entirely.

The presence of a cat at a marriage ceremony is said to bring the best of luck to both the bride and the groom in the years to come. It is for this reason that some superstitiously minded cat-lovers insist on bringing along the family cat with them to weddings.

To ensure a long and happy married life, a bride-to-be should feed a cat before her marriage ceremony commences. Nineteenth-century (or older) cat-folklore from Wales encourages girls to keep their cats well-fed and contented, which will prevent rain from falling on their wedding day.

In the thirteenth-century it was believed by some that after death, the souls of women who never married took possession

Cats, perhaps more than any other animal, play an important role in a wide
variety of superstitious beliefs and divinations concerning love and holy
matrimony.

of black cats. It is hardly coincidental that the only animal allowed in English convents during that era was the cat. (The
Ancren Riwle of the year 1205 stated: "Ye, my dear sisters, shall
have no beast but a cat.")

A Seafaring Cat Superstition

Sailors once believed that having a cat of any color or breed ac-
company them at sea offered supernatural protection against
shipwrecks, misfortune, and even death. Not to have a cat aboard
was to court with disaster and tempt fate! (Note: For additional
superstitions and omens connected with cats and those who sail
the seas, see the section on Weather Prognostications, page 99.)

Shape-Shifting

It is believed among a primitive Bengali tribe that certain women are capable of transforming their souls into black cats. If such a cat becomes physically wounded, the identical wound will appear upon the body of the women. And if the cat should be killed, the women will experience a similar death at the exact moment the cat dies.

Sun and Moon

A curious legend that dates back to ancient times is that male cats are ruled by the Sun and influenced by its solar energies, while female cats are ruled by the Moon and influenced by its lunar energies. This belief is rooted in the ancient linking of the cat to the great "heavenly couple" (the Sun and Moon) worshipped in many pagan religions of old.

Unexpected Callers

When a female cat washes her face in the evening, this is an omen that someone will soon pay an unexpected visit. To learn from which direction the visitor will arrive, observe the direction the cat first looks to after she finishes washing and this shall be the one.

A cat that washes its face and then puts its paw over its left ear is a sign that a visitor of the female gender shall soon arrive for a visit. Expect a male caller if the cat washes its face over its right ear.

If any cat (pet or stray) is observed washing itself in your doorstep, according to an old belief among some Christians, your house shall soon be visited by a clergyman.

Weather Prognostication

Ancient lore holds that the tail of a sleeping cat (especially a calico) can be used to predict the weather. If it is turned toward the direction of north or east, this indicates an approaching storm. But if it is turned toward the direction of south or west, pleasant weather is portended.

Fair weather is indicated when a cat washes itself in a normal manner; however, if it sits with its tail toward the fireplace, washes itself above the ears, or lies curled up with its forehead touching the ground, this is said to be a sure sign of a storm brewing. In some cases, a cat that sits with its back to the fireplace is an omen of chilly weather or a hard frost.

Wet weather is in the offing when a cat sneezes, licks its tail, or frolics with abandon. Stormy weather is indicated by a cat that scratches a table leg or washes vigorously behind its ears. In China it was once believed that the winking of a cat's eye was a sure sign of rain.

In New England (especially in the seacoast communities on Cape Cod) it was once believed that cats could conjure up a ferocious windstorm simply by clawing at a cushion or a carpet. Expect rain in the forecast if a cat washes its face in the parlor or sharpens its nails upon a fence, according to an old Yankee weather superstition from the state of Maine. New Englanders also believed that if a cat acted uneasy or in a strange manner, it was a sign of an approaching tempest. Throughout many regions of the world it was commonly believed that a great wind (particularly at sea) could be raised by trapping a cat in a cupboard or under a pot—a practice once common among the wives of sailors to keep their mates ashore.

Chinese seafarers believed that favorable winds were ensured if a cat was carried aboard ship, but if the cat acted unusually playful and frolicsome, this was taken as a sign of an impending gale. Many English sailors believed that if their wives' cats were contented, their luck would be preserved, and they would encounter only the fairest of weather while on their voyages. While it is generally regarded as good luck to have one or more cats on a ship, occult lore states that to throw a ship's cat overboard or mistreat it in any way will cause a great storm at sea.

Long ago in eastern Europe, it was a common belief among the peasantry that lightning bolts were produced by angels to drive out the demons that took possession of cats' bodies during thunderstorms. It was for this reason that cats were believed to attract lightning and were banished from Slavic houses at the onset of a storm.

Witches and the Devil

In the Middle Ages, many superstitious folks believed that black cats were demonical in nature, and many were thought to be the Devil in disguise. It was also believed that after seven years of service to a witch, a cat itself could become a witch, or even a devil, if it so desired. Closely related to this myth is the old Hungarian superstition that almost all cats turned into witches between the ages of seven and twelve years.

In parts of Europe it was once believed that kittens born in the month of May should be drowned to prevent them from becoming witches. (At one time, May was a time of year associated with witchcraft and all manners of evil—perhaps because it began with the old witches' Sabbat of Beltane and also the pagan feast of Floralia, which was celebrated in Rome.)

To prevent their cats from turning into witches or devils, superstitious people in the rural regions of eastern Europe often marked them with the symbol of the cross. Sometimes cross-shaped incisions were placed upon the bodies of newborn kittens with a blade dipped in holy water. The marking of crosses on cats was also believed to both protect and release them from any spells cast upon them by sorcerers. In Japan, the cutting off of a kitten's tail was once carried out to prevent it from turning into a demon when it reached maturity.

During the era of the Inquisition, it was commonly believed that witches' cats (familiars) fed on the blood or breast milk of their mistresses. They rose on broomsticks to the Black Mass, possessed the powers of transformation and invisibility, assisted

In some parts of the world it is believed that black cats bring bad luck to those whose paths they cross. However, in other parts of the world it is believed that black cats are lucky omens. (Photo by Gerina Dunwich)

witches and warlocks in the casting of wicked spells and sinister potions, and could only be destroyed by fire.

If a cat jumps over a corpse in its coffin, it is widely believed that the soul of the deceased will be claimed by the Devil, and in some cases, the corpse is doomed to forever walk the earth as one of the bloodthirsty undead. The leaping of a cat upon or over a corpse in its coffin is also said to portend dire misfortune or make blind the first unfortunate individual whom the cat jumps over afterwards, unless the cat is immediately caught and killed. Even in modern times, many people are uncomfortable with the thought of permitting a cat to be in the same room with a laid-out corpse or a person upon their deathbed. And the very sight of a cat (especially a black one) crossing the path of a funeral procession strikes immediate and unmeasurable terror within the hearts of the truly superstitious.

Beware of black cats that are seen on newly constructed bridges for they are sent by the Devil to claim the soul of the first person that crosses. This superstition was, at one time, widespread throughout much of Europe, and in some rural communities of the present day it continues to be told—especially whenever a new bridge is built.

7

Legendary Tails

Around the world curious legends and folktales about mysterious cats with supernatural powers abound. Many of these portray the cat as a diabolical creature, such as the legend of the black cat of the Isle of Skye who was actually a wicked sorceress in disguise, and the supposedly true story of the evil-natured supernatural cat that plagued the Hex Cat Farm in rural Pennsylvania until it was shot and killed by a golden bullet.

Cats have also been the popular subjects of many fairy tales and nursery rhymes, such as: The King O' the Cats (a folktale from Badenoch), "Puss-in-Boots," *The Cat in the Hat,* "The Owl and the Pussycat," *The White Cat,* and let us not forget the grinning Cheshire Cat of Lewis Carroll's *Alice in Wonderland.* Even the popular *Aesop's Fables* is no stranger to the charm and mysterious ways of the cat. (Aesop was said to have been a cat-lover, in case you had any doubts.)

In many parts of the world it was believed that cats were put on earth for the sole purpose of bringing the souls of the dead to the underworld. In some cases, cats emerged from the underworld to identify those who were wicked. One good example was Edgar Allan Poe's famous black cat, Pluto, who seemingly comes back from the dead to seek revenge against the cruel drunkard who mercilessly cut out one of his eyes with a penknife, slipped a noose about his neck, and then hanged him from a tree limb. In the story of *The Black Cat,* the cat's killer, in a rage of madness, murders his wife with an axe and then walls up her body in the cellar. Four days later, a party of policemen arrive to investigate the woman's strange disappearance. After a search of the premises turns up no clues, the officers are about to leave when they suddenly hear a sound similar to a crying baby followed by an inhuman wailing shriek coming from behind the cellar wall. Upon breaking it open, they discover within the foul-smelling tomb the decomposing corpse of the missing woman, and perched upon her bloodied head is the wailing, fiery-eyed black cat. Consigning his murderous master to the hangman, the feline clearly has the last laugh in this classic nineteenth-century tale.

Cat-Women

Folktales of women who transformed at night into cats and then returned at dawn in human form can be found in many countries throughout Europe. Cat-women often shape-shifted so they could sneak away from their husbands while they slept in order to meet their lovers in the dark shadows of the night or under the romantic silvery rays of the moon.

Some stories tell of cat-women who commit various crimes, such as theft or murder, while in the form of a cat. Whatever wounds afflicted upon them as a cat are said to remain on their bodies after turning back into human form. Quite often, this is the only way that a cat-woman can be detected. Belief in this old folk-legend no doubt led to the arrests and executions during the Burning Times of many innocent women who were unfortunate enough to be found to have upon their bodies a

A nineteenth-century illustration by Gerard Grandville

wound, scar, or strange mark located in the same place as a cat that had suffered an injury or an attack.

It was also believed that if a cat-woman was killed while in cat form, her body would change back into a woman upon the moment of death. If her body was not burned and her soul not properly put to rest, her restless spirit would return to haunt, or even take possession of, the living.

Venus and Aeluros

One of Aesop's fables is about a young man who unwisely falls in love with a cat and prays to Venus, the love-goddess, to change her into a woman so that he can make her his bride. The young man's prayer is answered by the good-natured goddess, and the cat is transformed before his very eyes into a beautiful young woman. But on their wedding night, the bride sees a mouse scurrying across the floor and springs from the bed to chase after it in a catlike fashion. Her lover, understandably upset that his lady, despite her beautiful human appearance, was still a cat in her heart, invokes the goddess with his tears. Venus, realizing that the magickal transformation was not such a wise idea, changes the woman back into a cat. (Perhaps what she should have done was change the young man into a tomcat and then everyone would have been happy . . . except, of course, the mouse!)

In a similar mythological tale, Venus transforms a cat into a woman of great beauty and calls her Aeluros. But after Aeluros angers Venus by contending with her for beauty, the goddess of love returns her to her first nature and sends her off to chase a mouse. (Incidentally, it is from the name *Aeluros* that the word for cat-lover, *ailurophile,* and the word for the fear of cats, *ailurophobia* is derived.)

Monster Cats

In Europe a number of legends exist from days of old about monster cats—the personified agents of evil—that appear out of the shadows of darkness. These frightful felines possess great powers and take the utmost delight in devouring their human victims. Often, they are slain by heroes who are courageous and pure of heart, such as in the cases of King Arthur and Saint Brendan, who both were forced to confront and conquer such beasts.

The moral of these stories is almost always the same: In the end, good always triumphs over evil—no matter what form it may take.

The Vampire Cat of Nabeshima

Monster cats can also be found in Japanese folklore, as an Oriental equivalent of the winged, fire-breathing dragons of western Europe. One legend, the vampire cat of Nabeshima, tells of an evil cat that kills a beautiful maiden by sinking its fangs into her throat and draining her of her life's blood. After burying the maiden's corpse, the vampire cat assumes the identity of the dead girl. She then bewitches the young handsome prince who had been in love with the maiden and drains him each night of his "vital essence" until he is weak and one step away from death. The prince's chief advisor, suspicious that the prince's mysterious illness is being caused by something supernatural, stands watch over the prince as he lies on his deathbed. To keep himself from falling asleep, the advisor cuts his own leg so that the pain will force him to stay awake and alert. When the vampire cat shows up for her nightly feeding, she is confronted by the chief advisor. Unable to place him under her evil spell, she flees to the mountains and tries to hide, but she is eventually hunted down and destroyed.

The Myth of Diana and Her Cat

Diana, an important deity to contemporary witches (as well as to the witches of old), was a moon goddess and the mother of Aradia. She was worshipped in ancient times by the people of Rome. Her Greek counterpart was the virgin-huntress and lunar goddess called Artemis.

According to mythology, Diana's twin brother, the sun god Apollo, was extremely proud of himself for creating the fearless and powerful lion. He sent his roaring, golden-maned beast to frighten his sister. Instead of being intimidated by her brother's ferocious creation, Diana responded by using her divine powers to make a miniature copy of it as a parody to ridicule her brother and his lion. (And in doing so, the domestic cat was created.) In other myths, Diana's cat was the cat-moon who hunted and devoured the gray mice of twilight each evening.

There is no doubt that the myths surrounding the lunar goddess and her cat are responsible in whole or in part for the cat's everlasting association with the moon and its feminine energies, its mystery, and its magick.

Artemis

The ancient Greeks believed that their beloved gods and goddesses were chased into the deserts of Egypt by Typhon, a grotesque monster with an unpleasant disposition, whom the typhoon (a hurricane) is named after. To escape from Typhon, the goddess Artemis transformed herself into a cat and hid safely within the moon. (Not surprisingly, her Roman counterpart, Diana, also had something to do with cats and the moon.)

The Demon Cat of Dublin

According to an old Irish folk-legend that continues to be told by County Dublin country folks, the father of one of the *Fortnightly* newspaper editors was sitting down to supper with his guest, the local priest, when the family cat entered the room and began eating. The priest, who was clearly appalled to witness a cat feed before Christians, uttered a prayer over the cat, and it instantly went up the chimney in a burst of flames. The cat's owner, angered by what he had just witnessed, threatened to have the priest arrested. Calmly, the priest asked his host if he would like to see his cat, and after the man answered affirmatively, the priest brought the cat up, covered with chains, through the rug on the hearth. The old man's face, which had previously been contorted by a look of anger, had now turned as pale as a ghost upon the realization that the cat whom he had loved and shared his home with was actually a demon cat—a creature born in the fires of Hell.

Christian Cat Legends

It has been said that the domestic cat did not exist in the Garden of Eden. The only felines that roamed freely there were lions, tigers, leopards, and panthers.

Cats were worshipped as pagan gods in ancient Egypt around the same time that the Bible was being written. Many historians believe this is why there is no mention of the cat anywhere to be found within the "Good Book."

Aboard Noah's ark, according to an old story, the number of rodents had multiplied to such an extent that the ark was overrun with vermin and the safety of all the living creatures onboard the ship was threatened. The lioness came to the rescue (in some versions of this story, it is the lion). After Noah had passed his hand three times over her head, she sneezed forth a frisky little cat who was more than happy to help reduce the out-of-control rat and mouse population that infested the ark.

According to an old legend from Italy, a mother cat gave birth to her young in the stable in Bethlehem at the same moment that Mary gave birth to the infant Jesus. In works of religious art, this cat is often portrayed with a cross on its back.

In another Italian legend, an imprisoned Saint Francis, while attempting to recite his prayers, is relentlessly attacked by hundreds of toe-nibbling mice dispatched by the Devil. But before the mice could get the best of him, he is saved by a cat that magickally springs from his sleeve and pounces upon its prey. The cat manages to catch all but two of the rodents, which save themselves by escaping through a hole in the wall. To this very day, according to the legend, cats can be found sitting patiently before holes in walls waiting for those last two mice to come out of hiding.

The patron saint of cats (as well as gardeners, travelers, and widows) is Saint Gertrude of Nivelles. She is said to be invoked by souls in purgatory, as well as by anyone plagued by mice. Saint Agatha, another saint connected with cats, was known as Saint Gato in the old province of Languedoc. *Gato* is the Spanish word for cat.

Other saints connected with cats include Saint Jerome (whose cat was said to be the companion of philosophers), and Saint Yves of Treguier (the patron saint of lawyers in Brittany, whose cat symbolized every wicked quality attributed to lawyers).

From a wood engraving by Thomas Bewick

In works of religious art, Saint Yves sometimes appears in the form of a cat.

An old fable from Russia tells of the cat and the dog who stand guard at the gates of Heaven. One day the Devil decides to sneak in by disguising himself as a tiny, inconspicuous mouse. He sneaks past the dog with the greatest of ease, but when he tries to sneak past the cat, who is a superior hunter, she pounces upon him without mercy and prevents him from slipping through the entrance to Paradise.

Witch-Cats of the Azande

For many centuries a primitive tribe known as the Azande have passed down from one generation to the next a legend of the most evil of all creatures—the witch-cat (a species of wild cat known as Adandara). Witch-cats are said to dwell in the bush, possess bright bodies and eerie glowing eyes, and haunt the night with their shrill, bansheelike cries, which are extremely unlucky for anyone to hear. Even more unlucky is to see a witch-cat, for to do so is almost always an omen of death.

Sometimes an unsuspecting woman is impregnated by a male witch-cat at night while she sleeps and ends up giving birth to kittens. Luckily for Azande women this does not happen with any frequency, for such kittens demand to be breastfed in the same manner as human infants . . . only their teeth and claws are very sharp!

The only tried and true way to ward off the influence of a witch-cat is to loudly blow on a magick whistle enchanted by a special spoken charm.

Felines and Fairy-Folk

It has been said that fairies are not very fond of cats, and if you wish to keep your home and yard free of fairies and their mischief, all you need to do is own a cat.

I hesitate to invest much belief in such old wives' tales simply because I know of many magickal folks who are both cat-lovers and cat-owners, and these individuals appear to have no shortage of fairy-folk in and around their homes.

Cats naturally possess a psychic vision that is greater than that of most humans. They can see things that the average person cannot see, such as ghosts and nature spirits. On more than one occasion I have seen witches' cats frolicking merrily, both indoors and out, with their magickal fairy playmates, and I know of other persons who have witnessed such delightful sights. I also have one good acquaintance who had previously never seen fairies or experienced fairy activity around his house until he and his wife added two cats to their family.

The connection between cats (as well as other animals) and the mysterious, invisible realm of the fairy-folk is one that is both age-old and great. Fairies possess an elemental nature that makes a large number of them the natural protectors and healers of animals (both domestic and wild), as well as of trees, flowers, and plants.

It is not uncommon for witches to call upon fairies when casting spells or performing certain rituals involving cats and other animals. Fairy magick is powerful energy, and humans who receive their blessings are extremely fortunate individuals indeed.

If your cat must be left by itself when you are called away, you may invoke the fairies to watch over the animal and keep it safe from harm and loneliness. These beneficial beings can also be called upon to protect and bless newborn kittens, cats with health problems, and cats that have wandered far from home and lost their way.

Fairies have also been known to assist witches and their familiars in the ancient and sacred art of divination. It is said that if a witch wishes to know things that are unknown, she should walk through a forest and ask the fairy-folk for their aid. (Communication between witches and fairies can be either verbal or telepathic.) They will supply the witch with the answer she seeks, but it will be in a symbolic form that must be properly interpreted like any other omen or sign. If such a symbol happens to be that of a cat, its basic divinatory meanings are: psychic powers and any or all things pertaining to the world of the occult.

You should always give sincere thanks to the fairies for their favors, both great and small, and be sure to leave little offerings for them outside your door or in places such as your backyard, a garden, a forest, or an open meadow. The customary offering is milk and honey, and the best times to leave it are at night (just before you go to bed) and on the first day of spring.

Of the hundreds of known fairy types throughout the world, the ones most associated with the protection and healing of animals are: the *Brown Men* (also called *Moor Men,* and found primarily in Cornwall, England), *Brownies* (nocturnal male fairies known to be extremely benevolent and generous), the *Dinnshenchas* (shape-shifting Irish fairies that guard cattle and protect human females), *Gnomes* (male dwarf fairies that are said to dwell in or beneath old oak trees), *Gruagach* (a solitary Scottish fairy said to appear in the form of an ugly and profusely hairy woman), the *Masseriols* (Italian male fairies that are often found on farms), *Twlwwyth Tegs* (friendly anthropomorphic

fairies said to dwell on fairy islands near the coast of Wales), the
Vasily (Russian fairies that dwell in barns and protect horses),
the *Vilas* (female woodland fairies that are partial to dogs),
and the *Zips* (male fairies from Mexico and Central America
that are known to protect wild deer and stags).

On the Isle of Man, there is said to exist a race known as
the *Tighe faeries*. They are related to the Brownies and are very
fond of all animals—except cats, which are their most feared
and hated of enemies. According to folklore, Tighe faeries come
at night to the homes of deserving humans who leave offerings
of food for them on the porch. While the human occupants
sleep, the fairies perform various household chores and then return to fairyland before the first rays of sunlight illuminate the
dawn. However, they never venture near houses that have cats
in or around them.

Recommended Fairy Books

A Witch's Guide to Faery Folk by Edain McCoy. St. Paul, Minn.:
Llewellyn Publications, 1997.

The Vanishing People: Fairy Lore and Legends by Katherine Briggs.
New York: Pantheon Books, 1978.

The World Guide to Gnomes, Fairies, Elves and Other Little People
by Thomas Keightley. New York: Avenel Books, 1978.

Fantastic People: Magical Races of Myth and Legend by Allan Scott
and Michael Scott Rohan. New York: Galahad Books, 1980.

The Enchanted World Series: Fairies and Elves. Alexandria, Va.:
Time-Life Books 1984.

The Cat and the Fiddle

Nearly everyone, both young and old, is familiar with the
popular nursery rhyme that starts out: "Hey diddle diddle, the
cat and the fiddle. . . ." This whimsical children's rhyme, which
first appeared in print in the year 1765, curiously links the cat

with the fiddle, as do many of the animal carvings found in English churches and cathedrals dating back to medieval times.

Interestingly, the musical instrument sacred to the Egyptian cat-goddess Bastet was the sistrum—an instrument with four strings like the fiddle. This strange coincidence raises the question: Could the cat and fiddle carvings found throughout old England possibly be linked to the cat-worship cult of ancient Egypt? Perhaps only Bastet, herself, knows for sure.

Elfin Cats

In the Highlands of Scotland, spine-tingling tales of elfin cats continue to be told, especially on dark, stormy nights when the wind moans like a restless spirit and the fire casts eerie shadows upon the hearth. These supernatural creatures, known as the Cait Sith (pronounced *cait shee*), are said to be the size of large dogs. They are always covered in black fur with white spots upon their chests. Their backs are arched like that of a Halloween cat, and the wailing sounds they emit at night are said to be blood-curdling.

Scottish legend holds that the Cait Sith are the most wicked of fairies in disguise, hungry for the chance to bring mischief and harm upon their unfortunate human victims. But some Highlanders believe that elfin cats are actually demons or evil witches in cat form.

Irish Cat Legends

Ireland, a country rich with folklore and a history of magick, is home to numerous cat legends and myths.

The tale of Irusan, the great King-Cat of Ireland, is mentioned in the old writings known as *The Proceedings of the Grand Bardic Academy*. Interestingly, Irusan's home was said to have been in the Knowth burial chamber in County Meath, and, according to Robert Graves (author of *The White Goddess*), an old Irish cat-cult existed around the same time as New Grange and was centered in County Meath at the same location where Irusan was said to have dwelt.

There exists an old Irish legend about a cat called "Little Cat" who guarded a treasure. This cat possessed great supernatural powers and did not take kindly to thieves. Foolish mortals who attempted to steal Little Cat's treasure were met with a fiery death, for the cat would magickally transform itself into pure flame and reduce them to a heap of smoldering ashes.

A legend of great antiquity tells of a mysterious island somewhere off the coast of Ireland that is home to a strange race of cat-people with human bodies and feline heads. Another account of cat-headed people can be found in Irish mythology in the tale of the hero Finn who battled a tribe of "cat-heads." These two stories most likely sprang from the days when Irish warriors of the king known as "Carbar of the Cat's Head" engaged in battle wearing helmets covered by the skins of wild cats.

In pre-Christian times, according to a legend from Clough, an oracular black cat sat upon a silver chair in a shrine located within a cave. She possessed the gift of prophecy and was sought by many who needed to know the future or receive advice from the gods. However, if a mortal attempted to trick the cat in any way, she would reply with a scornful answer like the Oracle of Delphi.

Demon cats abound in old Irish legend. Cu Chulainn, the Irish hero, was said to have been attacked one night by three demonic cats that vanished into thin air at the light of dawn, and Saint Brendan narrowly escaped the savage fury of a great "sea cat" while searching with his monks for the Land of Promise.

But perhaps the most well-known demon cat of all is the one that hails from the old legend about the fisherman's wife from Connemara who was determined to catch the black cat that would sneak in each night and gobble up the best of her fish. After several unsuccessful attempts, the woman finally trapped the cat and swatted it as hard as she could with a wooden stick. But instead of retreating into the night as most cats normally would, this one angrily spat fire and attacked the fisherman's wife, clawing her face and arms until she was covered in her own blood. She called the cat "a devil" and then threw a bottle of holy water at it. The demonic cat instantly turned into a cloud of black smoke with two glowing eyes, and then it disappeared, never to be seen again.

The Moon-Goddess Cat

A folktale dating back to pagan times has it that if a mother cat gives birth seven times (the first litter consisting of only one kitten; the second litter consisting of two; the third litter consisting of three; and so forth until the seventh litter brings a total of twenty-eight kittens), she is connected to the twenty-eight-day lunar month, and she is therefore a sacred moon-goddess cat.

The Cat-Stone

An old Japanese legend tells about a shape-shifting witch who haunted a posting station on the Tokaido road. Her home was nestled beneath a cluster of pine trees near the temple, and her favorite evil deed was to change herself into a cat and scare young women who came to the temple to recite prayers and present offerings to the god Buddha. One day, the witch's victims were avenged as she, by her own evil power, was permanently turned into a huge cat-shaped stone, which stands in Okabe to this very day.

The Proverbial Feline

"When the cat's away, the mice will play."

"A gloved cat catches no mice."

"The cat who frightens the mice away is as good as the cat who eats them" is an old proverb that hails from Germany.

"What is born of a cat will catch mice."

"A timid cat makes a bold mouse" is a proverb from Scotland.

"The borrowed cat catches no mice" is an old Japanese proverb, as is: "When the cat mourns the mouse, you need not take her seriously."

"A cat that is always crying catches no mice" is an Arab proverb, similar to one from Holland which states that "A cat that meweth catcheth few mice."

"A lame cat is better than a swift horse when rats infest the palace" is a proverb from China.

"It takes a good many mice to kill a cat" is an old Danish proverb.

"Against a good cat, a good rat."

"When the cat and mouse agree, the farmer has no chance."

"Don't wake a sleeping cat" is a French proverb, similar to the American saying: "Let sleeping dogs lie."

"Though the cat winks a while, yet sure she is not blind" is a proverb from England.

"Better to be the head of a cat than the tail of a lion."

"Cats have nine lives—three for playing, three for straying, and three for staying."

"They that are inclined to win the world must have a black cat, a howling dog, and a crowing hen."

"Touch not the cat but with a glove."

"A cat may look at a king" is an English proverb dating back to the seventeenth century. Another old proverb from England is: "Singing cats and whistling girls will come to a bad end."

"The cat is hungry when a crust contents her."

"An old cat eats as much as a young one."

"Every cat is honest when the meat's put away in the larder."

"It's easy to teach the cat the way to the churn" is an old Scottish proverb.

"All cats love fish but dislike getting their feet wet."

"The cat shuts its eyes when it steals the cream" is an old English saying that refers to a person who fails to see his or her own faults.

"The cat knows whose beard she licks" is a twelfth-century proverb from merry old England.

"A woman who dislikes cats will never marry a handsome man," according to an old Dutch proverb.

"He who takes good care of cats will have a pretty wife." However, according to an old French proverb: "A man who loves cats will marry an immoral woman."

To "let the cat out of the bag" is a popular American saying that means "to reveal a secret."

"Raining cats and dogs" is another popular saying in the United States, which is used to describe a heavy downpour or a severe storm.

Perhaps the most famous of all cat proverbs is: "Curiosity killed the cat, but satisfaction brought it back."

8

Astrology for Cats

Astrology is perhaps the most ancient of the occult sciences, and undeniably the most popular one in practice today. Astrology is used for character analysis, personality profile, daily guidance, and prediction. Its appeal is worldwide and its popularity continues to increase as more and more people are finding spiritual fulfillment in the New Age and alternative religions, and allowing their minds to open up to the metaphysical and mystical realms.

Astrology is especially important to those who follow the paths of Wicca and Neo-Paganism because the yearly spring and autumn equinoxes, and the summer and winter solstices (celebrated as the four Minor Sabbats) correspond with the Sun's entering of the astrological signs of Aries, Libra, Cancer, and Capricorn, respectively. The influence of the Sun in these signs has a significant impact on the changing seasons and their magickal vibrations.

Astrology is also an important aspect of the magickal arts. For example, working with the appropriate astrologically based oils and gemstones that correspond to the astrological position of the Moon will reward you with greater results when casting spells and performing rituals. In addition, the more a witch or neo-pagan works with the energies of the stars in magick and divination, the stronger his intuitive and clairvoyant powers naturally become.

As most people already know, there are twelve signs of the zodiac in Western astrology. The first one is Aries, followed by Taurus, Gemini, Cancer, Leo, Virgo, Libra, Scorpio, Sagittarius, Capricorn, Aquarius, and Pisces.

Aries, Leo, and Sagittarius are ruled by the element of Fire. Taurus, Virgo, and Capricorn are ruled by the element of Earth. Gemini, Libra, and Aquarius are ruled by the element of Air. And Cancer, Scorpio, and Pisces are ruled by the element of Water. The Fire element corresponds to the spirit and to all spiritual aspects of life. The Earth element is linked with the physical realm, stability, and human needs. The Air element corresponds to the intellectual aspects of life and also to communication, while the Water element is strongly connected to the emotional side of human nature, as well as to the psychic realms.

What is commonly known as basic sun sign astrology uses a person's birth sign to determine certain information such as personality traits, strengths, and weaknesses, and sometimes even physical characteristics.

Most people, witches and neo-pagans included, associate sun sign astrology with humans and human affairs only; however, the same twinkling stars that exert their mystical influence over the human race shine down upon our four-legged friends as well. If astrology can work for people, it also can work for cats (and other animals).

Every feline possesses a distinct personality that is greatly influenced by the astrological position of the Sun at the moment of its birth. A cat's sun sign can also give an indication of its temperament and the signs of humans and of other animals it is the most and least compatible with.

Putting together a horoscope for a cat is basically the same as doing so for a human. Both have an ascendant (also called a rising sign), twelve houses, ten planets, aspects, conjunctions, and so forth. The only difference between a cat's chart and a human's would be the way in which the horoscopes are interpreted.

For instance, the tenth house in a chart is primarily concerned with career: Whichever planet and sign are found there

(The New York Public Library Picture Collection)

have a major influence upon one's job aptitude, talents, and career direction. How then, you might be thinking, would something like this relate to an ordinary housecat's chart? Certainly most cats, with the exception of a few television stars like Morris, are not too concerned with having a career . . . at least not by what the human definition of a career is. But if we allow ourselves to look at the world from a cat's point of view, we would realize that to a cat such things as keeping a barn or house free of mice, guarding the territory against intruder cats and other strange animals, or simply just being a loyal and loving companion to its human master or mistress are indeed important jobs (or careers, if you will). These jobs have both challenges and rewards.

The Aries Cat
March 21–April 19

Aries is the first sign of the zodiac; therefore, it is not at all unusual for the Aries cat to want to be first in line for everything. Aries is ruled by the planet Mars (named after the ancient Roman god of war), which makes this sign fiery and aggressive.

Aries cats are by no means timid. Many possess a quick temper and a fighting spirit that often get them into more than their share of trouble. They don't always initiate a cat fight, but rarely will they back down from one if confronted or attacked by another animal—even one larger and more powerful than they are.

Cats born under the sign of Aries are adventurous by nature, curious, brave, and always on the lookout for something new and exciting to do. They require lots of exercise, and like their human counterparts, Aries cats enjoy being active. They love to play and be entertained for hours, and chances are that you will tire out before they do.

They are self-reliant and easily excitable. They usually get what they want. If they don't, they can make life miserable for their humans with uncooperative behavior and acts of spite, such as urinating on your brand new furniture or clawing apart the draperies.

The sign of the Ram rules the head, and Aries cats are prone to accidents that frequently result in head injuries. But they absolutely adore having their heads rubbed and scratched. This makes them purr loudly, and sometimes they will try to grab your hand and give you a love bite. Sometimes they get a trifle carried away, and once in awhile a Band-Aid will be required.

Aries cats are most compatible with humans and other animals born under the astrological signs of Gemini, Libra, Aquarius, Aries, Leo, and Sagittarius. The signs least compatible with Aries are the three Earth signs (Taurus, Virgo, Capricorn) and the three Water signs (Cancer, Scorpio, Pisces).

The Taurus Cat
April 20–May 20

Cats born under the sign of the Bull love food and comfort, and they are content with simple surroundings. However, they will not complain if you spoil them with luxuries as well. They fear the loss of security, which is typical of an Earth sign, and are creatures of habit. They quickly settle into a routine and become somewhat agitated when their daily schedules are disrupted. Therefore, in order to keep your Taurus cat happy, make sure you feed him at the same times each day. You will probably also notice that Taurean catnaps take place at the same time, same place each day right on schedule. Bull-cats love to sleep, and being ruled by the element of Earth, their favorite places to do so are on rocks and on the ground where they can tune into the healing energies of the planetary Mother.

Taurus cats are affectionate, patient, and mellow; however, they can be extremely stubborn when they want to be. If they should happen to develop any bad habits, it will be next to impossible to break them. So make sure they are properly trained and know right from wrong at the earliest age possible.

Taurus traditionally rules the throat and the neck, which makes Taurus cats very vocal. They love to be heard and will meow often, enjoying it immensely when you meow back to them. Their necks are very sensitive and they often object to wearing a collar—no matter how stylish or expensive it may be.

Taurus cats are most compatible with humans and other animals born under the astrological signs of Cancer, Scorpio, Pisces, Taurus, Virgo, and Capricorn. The signs least compatible with Taurus are the three Fire signs (Aries, Leo, Sagittarius) and the three Air signs Aquarius, Gemini, Libra.

The Gemini Cat
May 21–June 20

Like their human counterparts, Gemini cats are extremely talkative, meowing all the time. They always seem to have something to say—or maybe it's just that they like to hear the sound of their own voice. They get this trait from their ruling planet Mercury, which governs all forms of communication. They also love when you converse with them, but be warned that they are easily bored and after a few minutes of idle chitchat they will probably turn and walk away in search of something more stimulating to their feline senses, such as a buzzing housefly or a falling leaf that invites them to play. It is natural for Gemini cats to appear disinterested or even uninterested at times, and they can be more restless, fickle, and impatient than cats of other signs. Whatever you do, do not serve them their dinner late. They do not like being kept waiting at feeding time. Because of their restlessness, Geminis need variety and constant attention. They also like to be the center of attention as well. They are clever animals and more comfortable with change than the majority of cats born under different signs.

Being an Air sign, Gemini cats love the outdoors, the sunshine, and plenty of fresh air. This is not to say that a Gemini does not do well as a house cat. You may find, however, that once you let your Gemini cat out of the house, he will quickly change his mind and want to come right back in. After you let him in, he will quickly decide that he wants to go back out. Never try to figure out a Gemini!

The sign of the Twins rules the nervous and respiratory systems, which gives the Gemini cat his quick reflexes. However, it also makes him prone to nervous conditions.

Gemini cats are most compatible with humans and other animals born under the astrological signs of Aries, Leo, Sagittarius, Gemini, Libra, and Aquarius. The signs least compatible with Gemini are the three Water signs (Cancer, Scorpio, Pisces) and the three Earth signs (Taurus, Virgo, Capricorn).

The Cancer Cat
June 21–July 22

Under the planetary rulership of the Moon, the sign of Cancer is linked to the home, the family, the mother, and children. Therefore, Cancer cats do not mind being house cats and may even prefer it to being outdoors. If they are made into outdoor cats, they will most likely stay close to the house, seldom, if ever, venturing beyond their own backyards.

They are very attached to their human families and do quite well in homes where there are children. They possess a strong maternal instinct and will defend their kittens with tooth and claw. It is also not unusual for male Cancer cats to try and mother their young ones. They will diligently guard a box of kittens while the mother cat is away, and they may even jump inside of it to keep the kittens warm and feeling safe.

Cancer cats are animals that possess strong likes and dislikes. They are self-protective, sensitive, and moody—especially when the moon is full. Their feelings are easily hurt, and they are cautious and not very comfortable around strangers. They will often become over-possessive or greatly dependent, upon the people they love. Jealousy is a typical trait in a Cancer cat, so if you are showing more attention to another pet, do not be the least surprised if the Cancer cat retreats to its favorite hiding spot to sulk and give you the cold, silent treatment.

The tendency to collect things is another strong and typical Cancer trait, which applies to cats as well as to humans born under the astrological sign of the Crab. Whether it be old, chewed-up cat toys or little odds and ends from around the house, the Cancer cat will collect them and hide them somewhere like a secret stash.

Cancer cats are most compatible with humans and other animals born under the astrological signs of Taurus, Virgo, Capricorn, Cancer, Scorpio, and Pisces. The signs least compatible with Cancer are the three Fire signs (Aries, Leo, Sagittarius) and the three Air signs (Gemini, Libra, Aquarius).

The Leo Cat
July 23–August 22

Leo, the sign of the Lion, is the king of the jungle and a natural-born leader. Leo cats may be lionlike in their appearance or their behavior. Even a Leo cat of small physical stature will roar when it finds it necessary to do so.

Ruled by the element of Fire, Leo cats are not very fond of cold weather. They love the sun (the planetary ruler of their sign) and are more than content to curl up in a warm, sunny spot and snooze for hours upon end.

Around other cats, Leo is the one who is in charge; no ifs, ands, or buts about it. Generosity is a Leo trait, and they will often share their food, toys, or catch of the day with a feline friend. But brave-hearted Leo can also be a relentless enemy. You will find very few, if any, cowardly lions.

Like their human counterparts, Leo cats crave lots of love and attention. They are turned on by extravagance—gourmet cat food, a luxurious cat bed, a state-of-the-art litter box, a catnip-scented scratching post . . . well, you get the idea. But cat lovers of the world be warned: If you over-spoil your Leo cat, she will likely turn into an arrogant snob who will live only to impress the other cats in the neighborhood.

Leo cats are most compatible with humans and other animals born under the astrological signs of Gemini, Libra, Aquarius, Aries, Leo, and Sagittarius. The signs least compatible with Leo are the three Water signs (Cancer, Scorpio, Pisces) and the three Earth signs (Taurus, Virgo, Capricorn).

The Virgo Cat
August 23–September 22

Ruled by the planet Mercury and the element of Earth, the Virgo cat is one that is very fastidious and tidy. They will not tolerate a messy litter box and are uncomfortable in an unclean or overly cluttered environment. They take great pleasure in grooming themselves and are one of the few types of cats that don't mind getting a bubble bath and pedicure.

Loyalty is a Virgo trait and they choose very carefully those to whom they give their love and affection. It usually takes a while to gain a Virgo cat's trust, and if you hurt them or do something that makes them really angry, you will find that they are not animals that forgive and forget easily.

Cats that are born under the sign of the Virgin are extremely intelligent, analytical, and observant, just as their human counterparts are. Security is important to them, and they appreciate the comfort a warm, loving home has to offer.

Many cats can be fussy from time to time, but the Virgo cat takes the cake on this one! Cats of the sixth sign of the zodiac will also exhibit indecisive behavior from time to time, unable to make up their minds if they want in or out, canned food or dry, and so forth.

Virgo cats are most compatible with humans and animals born under the astrological signs of Cancer, Scorpio, Pisces, Taurus, Virgo, and Capricorn. The signs least compatible with Virgo are the three Fire signs (Aries, Leo, Sagittarius) and the three Air signs (Gemini, Libra, Aquarius).

The Libra Cat
September 23–October 22

Ruled by the planet Venus, Libra cats are graceful creatures that are usually mellow by nature. They are appreciative and they need to be appreciated as well. Pet them often and whisper in their ears how cute and how smart they are. Flattery will get you everywhere with a Libra cat.

Friendliness is a Libra trait, and most cats born under this sign get along with just about everyone. They are very social and charming, and they are more than willing to please. It is difficult not to get along with a Libra cat. Most of them possess an easy-going attitude and are easy to train. A harmonious environment where the energies are well-balanced is extremely important to both the feline and human Libras. They like to get involved in whatever activity is taking place at the moment, and most are very fond of music and watching television.

Libra cats can be fussy about what they eat, although to a lesser degree than the Virgo cat. They are often indecisive and are easily influenced by other cats, which may be either a good or not so good thing depending upon the type of company your cat keeps.

If unhappiness should strike, the Libra cat will likely compensate for it with bouts of gluttony. They also deal with stress in much the same fashion. They hate confrontation and would rather make love than war, or simply be left alone.

Libra cats are most compatible with humans and other animals born under the astrological signs of Aries, Leo, Sagittarius, Gemini, Libra, and Aquarius. The signs least compatible with Libra are the three Water signs (Cancer, Scorpio, Pisces) and the three Earth signs (Taurus, Virgo, Capricorn).

The Scorpio Cat
October 23–November 21

All cats possess strong intuitive powers; however, the Scorpio cat (along with the Pisces cat) are blessed with the greatest psychic sensitivity. The same applies to Scorpio and Pisces humans as well. The Scorpio cat always seems to know just exactly what you are thinking or feeling, and what your next move will be long before you make it.

Cats that are born under the sign of the Scorpion are naturally curious, jealous, suspicious, and very possessive over the humans they love. There is also a secretive nature to Scorpio cats and they seldom make their true feelings obvious. They are very sensitive, easily hurt, and known to be quite vengeful. (Hell hath no fury like an angry Scorpio cat!) If they feel that their humans have neglected or mistreated them, they will not curl up in the corner and quietly put up with it. Instead, they will delight in doing something they know will really get your day off to a bad start.

They possess strong likes and dislikes and are very influential over other cats. Scorpio is ruled by Mars (the same war-god planet that rules over the astrological sign of Aries). This makes Scorpios excellent fighters, and in a cat fight they can be extremely vicious.

Scorpio rules over the reproductive organs, but for a Scorpio cat, mating can often be a difficult tasks—especially for the female. But this is not to say that they do not find pleasure in procreation. Like so many of their human counterparts, Scorpio cats always seem to be in heat.

Scorpio cats are most compatible with humans and animals born under the astrological signs of Taurus, Virgo, Capricorn, Cancer, Scorpio, and Pisces. The signs least compatible with Scorpio are the three Fire signs (Aries, Leo, Sagittarius) and the three Air signs (Gemini, Libra, Aquarius).

The Sagittarius Cat
November 22–December 21

Sagittarius cats are independent creatures and they love their freedom. They love to explore and are always on the lookout for a new adventure. Like their extraverted human counterparts, they love playing and having fun. Competition and challenges are a real turn-on for them. They quickly grow bored with routine and are not bothered by changes in their environment the way many other cats are. Patience is not one of their virtues, and restlessness is their middle name.

Sagittarius cats, unlike those born under the sign of Virgo, are not known for their neatness. They will often kick their gravel out of the litter box and spill their food all over the floor. It's in their nature and scolding them or attempting to train them to act otherwise is futile. However, if a Sagittarius cat has a Virgo rising, he will probably be more meticulous.

Cats born under the sign of the Centaur-Archer can be somewhat moody and are prone to accidents. They love to do cute things to make you laugh, and they thrive on being the center of attention.

Sagittarians also love to take chances. The human variety find stimulation in such things as gambling and daredevil sports, while the feline risk-takers like to test their nine lives by seeing if they can outrun the next door neighbor's attack dog, snatch a mouse away from a gang of ruffian alley cats, and other games of chance.

Sagittarius cats are most compatible with humans and animals born under the astrological signs of Gemini, Libra, Aquarius, Aries, Leo, and Sagittarius. The signs least compatible with Sagittarius are the three Earth signs (Taurus, Virgo, Capricorn) and the three Water signs (Cancer, Scorpio, Pisces).

The Capricorn Cat
December 22–January 19

The element of Earth makes the Capricorn cat laid-back and earthy. Like the Goat that symbolizes their sign, they like their surroundings to be quiet and peaceful. Loud noises make them nervous, and when human strangers invade their home territory, they become quite shy and may even retreat to a quiet, secluded hiding place to be alone. Strange animals are always approached with the utmost caution. Goat-cats like stability and have a strong fear of insecurity, which are typical traits of an Earth sign. For a loyal pet, your best bet is a Capricorn.

Being solitary is no problem for Capricorn cats. They like when you leave for work so they can have the house to themselves. Capricorns are leaders, not followers. If there are other cats in the family, the Capricorn cat will most likely be the dominant figure. But with Fire sign cats (especially Leos) the Capricorn cat is likely to encounter a power struggle. The Lion may prove to be the king of the jungle in the long run, but the Capricorn cat will never give up trying for first place. He is determined, above all else.

Capricorn cats often prefer the quiet activity of gazing out a window or being curled up in front of a crackling fireplace to roughhousing. They also adore rocking chairs. But every now and then boredom sets in and they need to run a little wild until they get it out of their systems, which usually doesn't take very long.

The sign of the Goat is also the sign of the climber, and Capricorn cats love climbing things. Whether it is a tree in the front yard or the bookcases in the den, they will scale heights with great skill and determination. Capricorns know what they want, and they know how to get it. It may take them awhile, but once they reach the top (which is every Capricorn's goal), you will probably need to call the fire department to get them down.

The Capricorn cat is most compatible with humans and other animals born under the astrological signs of Cancer, Scorpio, Pisces, Taurus, Virgo, and Capricorn. The signs least compatible with Capricorn are the three Fire signs (Aries, Leo, Sagittarius) and the three Air signs (Gemini, Libra, Aquarius).

The Aquarius Cat
January 20–February 18

Aquarius cats are extremely independent and their freedom is just as important to them as their food and water. They do not like to be cooped up inside for long and resent being put on a leash or imprisoned in a portable travel kennel. They have a rebellious streak, are friendly animals, and adapt rather quickly to changes. They are curious by nature, oblivious to the old saying that curiosity killed the cat. However, the vast majority of Aquarian cats prefer to observe rather than participate.

The planet Uranus, which rules the sign of the Water Bearer, makes the Aquarius cat unpredictable. However, if he is placed under a great deal of stress, he will most likely respond by becoming antisocial and giving you the silent treatment. If his rising sign is Aries, or if his natal chart has a lot of planets in Aries, he will be temperamental. If his chart shows planets in Scorpio, his reaction to stress will be spiteful.

Aquarius is the sign of the mind, and cats born under this sign are rather intuitive. They are also highly intelligent. It is easy to train an Aquarius cat because they are fast learners. They pride themselves on being the geniuses of the cat world.

Do not become alarmed if your Aquarius cat displays some strange behavior (i.e., acts out of the ordinary) from time to time. In most cases this is perfectly normal. Uranus is a wild and crazy planet, and eccentricity is the result of its influences.

The Aquarius cat is most compatible with humans and animals born under the astrological signs of Aries, Leo, Sagittarius, Gemini, Libra, and Aquarius. The signs least compatible with Aquarius are the three Water signs (Cancer, Scorpio, Pisces) and the three Earth signs (Taurus, Virgo, Capricorn).

The Pisces Cat
February 19–March 20

Ruled by the planet Neptune, Pisces is the last sign of the zodiac. It is also the most psychic, and this gives the Pisces cat a strong intuitive sixth sense. In addition, Pisces is the most emotional sign of the zodiac, next to Cancer and Scorpio. This is the reason that many Pisces cats tend to be hypersensitive, moody, and even temperamental at times.

Although many Pisces cats are normally timid, shy, and introverted, they are friendly and get along well with other animals. They grow restless very easily and love to roam from place to place by the light of the silvery moon.

Pisces rules the feet, which gives the sign of the Fishes their desire (or perhaps their need) to constantly be on the go. It also gives them sensitive paws that are prone to tenderness and occasional injuries.

Food is important to the Pisces cat and their favorite cuisine is, of course, seafood. If they are not fed on time, they will become grumpy. Pisceans, both feline and human, can be very impatient and whine when they cannot have their ways. But once they mellow out, they will cuddle up in your lap and shower you with affection.

Cats that are born under the sign of Pisces are naturally mysterious and mystical. Many are attracted to witches and others who practice, or take a strong interest in, the magickal arts. They have dreamy eyes, and if you gaze into them long enough you may feel like you are looking into the windows to another world.

The Pisces cat is most compatible with humans and other animals born under the astrological signs of Taurus, Virgo, Capricorn, Cancer, Scorpio, and Pisces. The signs least compatible with Pisces are the three Fire signs (Aries, Leo, Sagittarius) and the three Air signs (Gemini, Libra, Aquarius).

Lunar Influences

If you are considering buying a cat or obtaining one from an animal shelter that requires an adoption fee, the ideal time to do so, according to astrologers, is when the moon is new or in its first quarter, and in any astrological sign, except for Scorpio and Pisces.

Cat training, which isn't always an easy thing to do, is said to be less difficult to accomplish when it is started while the moon is new or in the astrological sign of Taurus. This includes litter-box training of kittens, and the teaching of good behavior, as well as tricks, to young cats (or older ones if you are a person with an endless supply of patience!). Other moon signs that help make cats and other animals easier to handle are Cancer, Libra, and Pisces. If you can, avoid trying to train your cat to do anything when the moon is full. You will only be wasting your time. And also take care not to handle wild cats during this lunar phase unless you fancy scratches and bite marks upon your flesh.

The best time to plant catnip, according to the laws of lunar gardening, is when the moon is positioned in Libra or any of the three signs ruled by the element of Water: Cancer, Scorpio, and Pisces. Fertilize when the moon is in Cancer, Scorpio, Pisces, Taurus, or Capricorn. Weed and spray for pests when the moon is in its fourth quarter and in what is known as a barren sign. These are Aries, Gemini, Leo, Virgo, Sagittarius, and Aquarius. Water your catnip when the moon is in Cancer, Scorpio, or Pisces (the three Water signs of the zodiac), and harvest when the moon is full—unless, of course, your cat (or one of the neighborhood kitties) decides that an early catnip harvest is in order, in which case she will let you know by rolling around in, and chewing up, your prized catnip patch.

The Year of the Cat

If you were born in the year 1903, 1915, 1927, 1939, 1951, 1963, 1975, or 1987, your birthday falls in the Year of the Cat.

In traditional Vietnamese astrology, the Cat (which corresponds to the Rabbit in Chinese astrology) is one of the twelve zodiac animals whose characteristics infuse an astrological cycle of the years and control the fortunes of those who are born under their signs.

Interestingly, in Chinese horoscopes, the Cat replaces the Rabbit in the astrology system only in North China because the word *rabbit* possesses an insulting meaning in that part of the country.

According to a Chinese legend that dates back to around A. D. 600, after the establishment of Buddhism, the great Buddha invited the Cat, along with the Rat, Ox, Tiger, Rabbit, Dragon, Snake, Horse, Goat, Monkey, Rooster, Dog, and Pig, to visit him so that he could name the years after them in order to make it easier to remember the Sexagenary Cycle. The cat fell asleep and did not make the journey with the other twelve animals, and therefore no year was ever named after him in traditional Chinese astrology.

In a similar legend, Buddha had invited all the animals of China to participate in a race and promised that the first twelve winners would be honored by having one year named after each of them. Prior to the race, the Cat and the Rat were the best of friends and even snuggled up together in the same cozy bed. Before sleeping they made a promise to each other: The one who woke up from his nap first would awaken the other so he would not miss the race and lose out on the honor of having a year named after him. The Rat was the first to rouse from his sleep, but he did not wake up his feline friend as he had promised. Instead, he dashed off to the race and became one of the twelve animals of the Chinese zodiac. By the time the poor sleeping cat had awakened from his catnap on the warm, cozy bed, the race was over and the twelve winners were the Rat, Ox, Tiger, Rabbit, Dragon, Snake, Horse, Goat, Monkey, Rooster, Dog, and Pig. Understandably furious at the Rat for breaking his promise, the Cat vowed vengeance. And this is why, according to the ancient legend, the Cat and the Rat are enemies to this very day.

Persons whose birthdays are in a Year of the Cat are said to be ambitious folks who are not afraid of hard work. They are careful when they need to be, intelligent, well-mannered, virtuous, and quite clever. They love tradition and being outdoors, and many possess great talent where music is concerned. Cat people, like the animal that symbolizes their birth year, have a certain air of refinement and a bit of mystery about them.

In the romance department, the Cat is said to be most compatible with persons born in the Year of the Snake (1905, 1917, 1929, 1941, 1953, 1965, 1977, 1989), the Goat (1907, 1919, 1931, 1943, 1955, 1967, 1979, 1991), the Pig (1911, 1923, 1935, 1947, 1959, 1971, 1983, 1995), the Ox or Buffalo (1901, 1913, 1925, 1937, 1949, 1961, 1973, 1985, 1997), the Dog (1910, 1922, 1934, 1946, 1958, 1970, 1982, 1994), and the Cat. The least compatible of the animal years with the Cat are the Rat (1900, 1912, 1924, 1936, 1948, 1960, 1972, 1984, 1996), the Dragon (1904, 1916, 1928, 1940, 1952, 1964, 1976, 1988, 2000), the Horse (1906, 1918, 1930, 1942, 1954, 1966, 1978, 1990), the

Tiger (1902, 1914, 1926, 1938, 1950, 1962, 1974, 1986, 1998), the Rooster (1909, 1921, 1933, 1945, 1957, 1969, 1981, 1993), and the Monkey (1908, 1920, 1932, 1944, 1956, 1968, 1980, 1992). However, some Chinese astrologers believe that the Monkey is a good match for the Cat.

Cats are loving and loyal to their mates, but they can also be oversensitive, aloof, and sometimes downright devious! Cat people also tend to have an overabundance of energy and are prone to nervous conditions if they allow problems (even the smallest ones) to get the best of them. Many are psychic-sensitive and can sense danger before it strikes. Often psychic warnings come to them in the form of dreams.

The final year of the twentieth century (1999) is a Year of the Cat, which seems to be appropriate. Cats are curious by nature and intrigued by the unknown. And as the twentieth century draws to its final twelve months, the influence of the Cat will be evident throughout the world as the human race awaits the coming millennium and its unknown, with an abundance of cat curiosity and intrigue.

In the twenty-first century, the Year of the Cat occurs in the following years: 2011, 2023, 2035, 2047, 2059, 2071, 2083, and 2095.

A seventeenth-century engraving from the *Recueil des plus illustres proverbes*

Astrological Magick for Cats

Cat amulets were all the rage in ancient Egypt. They were worn not only by kings and commoners alike, but also by cats. They were believed to be extremely powerful and were used for good luck, promoting fertility, and protection against evil, among other things.

A cat-shaped amulet (available in many occult shops and mail-order catalogues) that has your cat's astrological sign painted or engraved upon it works well to keep your cat protected from harm. It should be attached to your pet's collar (especially if it is an outdoor cat) or placed somewhere in the home, such as underneath the cat's bedding or feeding bowl.

Astrological amulets should always be cleansed of any negative vibrations before you use them in a magickal fashion. To do this, simply hold the amulet under cool running water for several minutes as you chant:

> Negative vibrations vanish,
> Evil spirits, thee I banish,
> Positive vibrations flower,
> Charge this amulet with thy power.

You can also clear negative vibrations from an amulet by burying it in a small cauldron or other container filled with salt. (Note: Some practitioners of the magickal arts prefer to work only with sea salt and will not use ordinary table salt in any of their rituals.) The amulet must stay in the salt for at least three days and three nights, and preferably when the moon is in her waning phase. If the amulet is heavily imbedded with negative or evil energies, the cleansing period will have to be increased to nine days and nights.

Whenever performing magick on your cat (such as healing work, fertility-increasing spells, and so forth), you will obtain greater results by using the oils, candle colors, gemstones, and other magickal paraphernalia that correctly correspond to your cat's astrological sign. A list of magickal correspondences can be found in most contemporary books on Wicca and the spell-casting arts. And always be sure to perform your spell-work during the proper lunar phase—a new moon for beginnings; waxing for attracting; full for psychic, fertility, and power matters; and waning for banishing. The dark of the moon is seldom used by modern witches; however, some practitioners of sorcery have been known to utilize this lunar time for the casting of black magick.

Your cat's birthday is a special occasion and an important astrological time, for on this day the planets return to the same positions they were in at the time when the cat was born. Birthdays (also known to astrologers as "solar return days") are ideal times for performing blessings for your cat, and spells to ensure her good luck, health, and longevity.

If you do not know your cat's birth date, you may be at least able to guess its astrological sign by matching her personality traits to those of the basic sun sign personality. For instance, if she is a fighter she may be born under the astrological sign of Aries. If she is sensitive, moody, and very attached to being in the house and around the family, chances are good that she was born a Cancer.

If that still has you puzzled, you might be able to find out the date, or at least part of it, by using a dowsing pendulum, a Ouija board, or even dream work. You do not have to be a super psychic in order to use divinatory methods. However, if you are gifted with clairvoyant perception, your results will naturally be more favorable.

But if that doesn't work for you either, then don't despair. Just be sure to give your cat plenty of love 365 days of the year and that should do the trick. Remember, love is the greatest magick there is!

9

Cat Cures

Cats have been highly valued by folk healers and practitioners of the magickal arts alike since ancient times. They have been utilized in a number of ways to treat or ward off nearly every disease known to mankind, and hardly any part of the cat's anatomy has been overlooked as possessing curative or magickal powers. Incredibly, even its dung and urine were accredited with miraculous healing powers. In Victorian-era England, cat's dung and urine was made into an ointment with powdered mustard seed, onion juice, and bear's grease (the melted fat of a bear), and prescribed regularly by physicians as a cure for baldness and alopecia. (It would be a fair guess to assume that this unusual, if not utterly disgusting, ointment was applied externally.) Obviously the cat-dung concoction had little, if any, positive results, and as modern medicine grew more sophisticated, this and other such cat-remedies were demoted to the ranks of superstition and quackery.

Within this chapter you will discover a curious collection of cat cures from the past. Some are of a magickal nature, while others are straight out of the textbooks of early medicine. And many are, without a doubt, so unbelievably ludicrous that they will leave you amazed, hysterical with laughter, or possibly even sick to your stomach! The cat cures found in this chapter are included here for historical and educational purposes only, as well as for their evident entertainment value. They are by no means intended for actual use!

No modern witch would ever consider doing harm to a cat, or any other living thing for that matter, because it is against our Rede, which states: "An' it harm none, do what ye will." (And even if you are not a witch and do not live by the Rede, it is still very bad luck to harm or kill a cat, and not a very fitting way to treat a descendant of an attendant of the great goddess Bastet.)

Japanese folk healers claim that cats are instrumental in curing such ailments as epilepsy, melancholia, and stomach spasms. All cats are believed to possess healing qualities of one sort or another; however, black cats supposedly possess it in greater abundance.

Interestingly, in neighboring China, the black cat is regarded by most who subscribe to superstition as the harbinger of illness and poverty. This belief can also be found in the countries of Germany and France, where black cats were at one time caged and burned alive in the belief that they were witches in disguise. An old German cat superstition has it that the act of a black cat jumping onto the bed of an ill person is a certain omen of death for that individual, as is the sight of two cats fighting in the presence of a sick or elderly person. And, according to an old folk-belief from Normandy, if a black cat crosses a person's path in the moonlight, that unlucky individual will probably fall victim to an epidemic before the year is through.

In Holland, many people once believed that inflammations could be cured by applying the skin of a freshly killed cat. Dutch folk healers also employed cat skin to treat a number of other ailments ranging from hives to sore throats.

(The New York Public Library Picture Collection)

It was once thought that a sick person could be cured of whatever ailment was troubling her by first washing and then throwing the dirty bathwater over a cat. Somehow this was supposed to transfer the patient's disease to the poor, unsuspecting cat, which would then take the disease from the house as it made a mad dash for the outside. (It is a well-known fact that the vast majority of cats are not partial to water and absolutely despise getting their fur wet. So if you try this, chances are that you will be no better off afterwards and your cat will not be a very happy camper!)

Cat's Blood

Many folk healers from around the world have long believed that the blood of a cat can successfully cure hives, in addition to eradicating "worms in the nose" and in other parts of the human body.

To cure what was once known as the "falling sickness," Victorian-era physicians recommended a bizarre remedy consisting of the "blood of a bore-cat's tail, salt of man's skull, and powdered ox horns." Bearing more resemblance to a witch-doctor's potion than to a dose of respected medicine, this concoction probably tasted terrible and worked poorly.

Folk healers in the past claimed that injuries sustained by a fall would heal faster if the patient sucked the blood out of a freshly amputated tail of a male cat. Equally as bizarre was the old notion that drinking a glass of red wine mixed with blood from a cat's ear could serve as a cure for pneumonia.

In some parts of the British Isles, it was once believed that the blood of a black cat contained the miraculous power to heal any flesh wound immediately upon contact. The trick behind this was to dip a raven's feather into the blood and then lay it upon the open wound as a powerful (but now long-forgotten) magickal incantation was recited by the healer.

Old-Fashioned Gout Remedies

Cat's grease mixed with palm oil and oil of aniseed was once hailed as a surefire treatment for gout. It was also used to dissolve tumors, relieve pain, and treat nodes (hard swellings or small protuberances) in the skin.

The flesh of a cat, especially a wild cat, was reputed to be another cure for gout at one time. The way in which it was used was as follows: The flesh was first salted, beaten until tender, and then carefully applied to the affected area.

Other medicinal uses for cat flesh included treating hemorrhoids, relieving toothache, easing the pain of rheumatism, and drawing out thorns from the body.

Remedies for Bleeding

If you were unfortunate enough to suffer a nosebleed in olden times, it is very possible that the village wise woman would have staunched it by inserting a cat's tail up your nostril. As ridiculous as this type of cure may sound, this practice was at one time common throughout many parts of Great Britain.

Wounds were once dressed with a preparation made from a cat that had been boiled in olive oil.

Consumption

Long ago in many parts of the southern United States, the disease known as consumption was supposedly cured by the eating of a special gravy made from a stewed black cat. The exact recipe for preparing such a cat gravy is not known, which is probably for the best. ("Consumption" is an old-fashioned term for pulmonary tuberculosis—an infectious disease of both humans and animals caused by tubercle bacilli.)

Liver and Gall

Some physicians of old were known to prescribe a mixture of powdered cat's liver, borax, bayberry roots, powder of elecampane, and other ingredients to treat gravel and correct problems in urinating.

For "bringing away birth and after birth," as well as for extracting moles, a pessary made from cat's gall, aloes, and musk was said to do the trick.

A Popular Spell for Curing Warts

It is quite common for witches to be portrayed in fairy tales as old hags with unsightly warts upon their noses and chins. However, it is doubtful that there were many real-life witches who were afflicted with them because, according to occult folklore, they have known since olden times how to use the tail of a cat to remove warts in a magickal fashion.

The treatment is quite simple and consists of rubbing the wart with the tail of a tortoiseshell (calico) tomcat. However, this method of wart removal is said to work only when it is performed during the month of May. If carried out in any other month of the year, its magickal power will be ineffective. And, if you are considering trying this old witches' wart-curing remedy for yourself, it is only fair to warn you that male tortoiseshell cats are extremely rare and difficult to come across.

In the Ozarks region of the United States, backwoods folk healers known as "power doctors" have long used cats in the following manner to "charm off" warts: First, the wart must be rubbed upon the fur of a black cat, which must then be killed. (It is important to use a black cat. If a cat of any other color is used, according to power doctors, the spell will not take effect.) The animal's lifeless body should then be taken to a cemetery after the sun has set and laid upon the grave of a man or woman who has been buried that same day. The way in which this spell supposedly works is as follows: As the cat's body (which the wart has been magickally transferred to) decomposes, it causes the wart to disappear. And if the person whose grave the cat is placed upon was one who led "a wicked life," it will cure the wart even faster.

A Remedy for Croup

The blood of a black cat has long been considered an effective remedy for croup, especially by folk healers of Pennsylvania hex-craft.

In the middle of the nineteenth-century, a Pennsylvania woman was publicly accused of practicing the "black art of Witchcraft" after numerous people witnessed her quick and successful curing of a child's croup by administering three drops of blood from a black cat. This case was mentioned in John Jennings's late nineteenth-century book, *Domestic and Fancy Cats;* however, the fate of the woman and her black cat was not disclosed.

Another outrageous folk remedy for treating croup calls for consuming a mixture of wine and cat excrement. (It is not clear whether the wine should be red or white, or an imported or domestic variety. Nor is it known from what color, breed, or gender of cat the excrement should be obtained.)

Diseases of the Eye

A popular remedy in the Middle Ages for treating diseases of the eye called for the head of a black cat to be burned into powder in an earthen pot. The powder would then be blown through a quill into the affected eye of the patient three times a day until the eye was healed of its malady.

A similar remedy for blindness, according to William Salmon's *The English Physician,* requires the ashes of a cat's head to be mixed with honey and "white vitriol in fine powder." This "balsam," as it was called, would then be applied to the eyes thrice daily.

Another remedy for treating blindness and dimness of sight called for honey and the gall of a cat. Together these two ingredients would be mixed and then used as a collyrium to wash the eyes.

The tail of a black cat was also believed to possess curative powers in treating such eye ailments as sties, inflammations, poor vision, eye pain, and even blindness. According to occult tradition, a single hair must be plucked from the cat's tail on the first night of the full moon, and then drawn across the eyelid nine times.

The belief in, and practice of, using a black cat's tail to treat eye diseases and ailments continues in various parts of the world today, including many rural regions of the United States. It remains especially popular among practitioners of Hoodoo in the southern states, and those who practice the art of hex-craft (also known as powwow) in Pennsylvania's Dutch country.

To Ward Off Illness

An old witches' spell that was once believed to keep all members of a household free from illness of any kind called for the tail of a black cat to be cut off with a blade anointed by the oils of frankincense and myrrh, and then buried underneath the doorstep of the home. When carried out on Beltane (an important witches' Sabbat celebrated on the first day of May), the potency of this spell is said to be greatly increased.

Black cats' tails have also been used by Hoodoo practitioners as good-luck charms and as magickal amulets to break curses and protect against the evil eye. However, it should be noted that cats tend to be quite fond of their tails and will not take very kindly to parting with them.

Pagan and New Age Remedies for Cats

The first part of this chapter examined the numerous, and often cruel and bizarre, ways in which cats have been used since ancient times to heal or prevent illness in humans. The remainder of this chapter is devoted to the healing of cats and the various methods used today by many pagans, modern witches, and individuals who incorporate the ways of the New Age into their lifestyles. These alternative and natural healing methods include herbal cures, gemstone therapy, and spell-craft.

Natural remedies for cats, which were commonly used in a by-gone era, have once again found popularity among cat-lovers throughout the world. Many folks are finding herbs and herbal-based products to be environmentally friendly and safer to use, yet just as effective, as store-bought pet products containing toxic chemicals.

Fleas

For the treatment of fleas, bathe your cat once a month when the moon is waning, using a natural pet shampoo containing flea-repellent herbs. Add a teaspoon of eucalyptus oil to the bathwater before putting the cat in it. Ruled by the Moon and the element of Water, this oil will add flea-killing power to the cat's bathwater, as well as healing energies for the body, mind, and spirit.

Another natural way to help control fleas is to add a bit of brewer's yeast or garlic to your cat's daily food. Fleas are known to be repelled by the smell and taste of these two things. You can also rub some brewer's yeast into your cat's fur, or use a natural flea powder containing such ingredients as citronella, eucalyptus, pennyroyal, rosemary, rue, or wormwood. (Caution: Use flea powders sparingly if they contain pennyroyal or powdered tobacco. Large quantities of these herbs can have a toxic effect on both animals and humans.)

Sprinkle a few drops of undiluted essential oil of cypress (ruled by the planet Saturn and the element of Earth) on your cat's bedding to help control fleas where your cat sleeps. Repeat once a week, or as often as needed.

Ear Mites

Another problem that commonly affects cats, especially outdoor ones, is the ear mite. To treat an infestation, mix one-half ounce of almond oil (ruled by the planet Mercury and the element of Air) and four hundred international units of Vitamin E in a dropper bottle. Put a few drops inside each ear to smother the mites. Gently massage the oil in, and then carefully clean out the cat's ears with a cotton swab.

Do this once a day for three consecutive days, wait three days, and then repeat the procedure. Note: Be sure to keep the oil mixture refrigerated to avoid spoiling, and gently warm it before each use.

Bee Stings

For bee stings and other insect bites, remove the stinger (if there is one) from the cat's skin and apply a dab of fresh aloe vera gel to the afflicted area. It is cooling and soothing, and can be used on other animals and humans as well. Aloe vera gel, which is also excellent for treating minor burns, can be purchased in most health food stores or easily obtained by cutting a small piece off of an aloe vera plant and then squeezing out the gel.

Healing With Crystals

To promote general good health in your cat or to help speed up his recovery from an illness or injury, many New Age healers recommend keeping a quartz crystal in the cat's nonmetallic water bowl. It is said that this stone will not only neutralize any psychic impurities in the water, but charge it with invisible, yet potent, energies for healing as well.

A healing quartz crystal can also be placed directly upon a cat's body or attached to its collar like an amulet to balance and realign any inharmonious energies.

When placed over an injured body part, the vibrations of a quartz crystal is believed by many to actually speed up the healing process. However, in the event of any serious injury or illness, it is recommended that you contact a qualified veterinarian without delay!

After a sick or injured cat has been healed, it is important that you cleanse the quartz crystal of whatever negative vibrations it may have absorbed. This can easily be done by soaking the crystal for twenty-four hours in a glass bowl filled with enough salty water to completely cover the stone. When done, remove the crystal from the water, dry it, and then allow it to rest beneath the golden rays of the sun from sunrise to sunset. Solar energies are beneficial for helping to recharge the crystal. (Note: Sunlight is good for recharging healing crystals; however, crystals that are used for divinatory purposes, such as crystal balls and dowsing pendulums, should always be recharged by the rays of moonlight and never exposed to the sun.)

Chakra Healing

Chakras have been described as "spinning vortexes of energy." They are located within our etheric bodies, and serve to connect the physical and the nonphysical self. All humans and animals are said to possess seven major chakras, which correspond to a different anatomical region and its related organs. They are invisible to the naked human eye; however, some gifted healers are able to perceive them through clairvoyant talents.

It is believed that the chakras play an important role in all levels of health (physical, mental, and emotional), as well as in the development of one's spirituality. If one or more of the chakras should become blocked by a buildup of negative energies, their natural balance becomes disturbed. Their rotation slows down and, as a result, they have an adverse influence upon the body functions they relate to.

Chakra healing clears the blockages that result in unhealthy chakras, and it stimulates their energy-processing rotation. There are various methods of chakra healing, but the one that incorporates the use of powerful healing gemstones (outlined below) is perhaps the most popular among the vast majority of New Agers and magickal folks today.

To perform a chakra healing on your cat, it is extremely important that the animal be completely at ease. (A nervous, frightened, or angry cat does not make a good patient!) Hold the cat in your arms and gently stroke its fur as you speak softly to it, reassuring it and expressing your love and concern. Continue doing this until the cat purrs and appears to be in a relaxed state. Now take the appropriate gemstone (see the list of chakras below) and place it over the chakra that needs healing work. Hold the gemstone in place for as long as possible while you visualize in your own way the healing process taking place. If you wish, you may also pray to the deity of your choice to send divine healing energy to the sick or injured cat.

The following are the seven major chakras, the body parts that they govern, and the healing gemstones that relate to their particular color rays.

First: Base Chakra

Color ray: RED

Located at the base of the spine, this chakra (also known as *muladhara*) relates to the following parts of a cat's body: the large intestine, back legs and feet, rectum, and tail. It also influences a cat's nature, taste, and sense of smell. The gemstones traditionally used for healing this chakra are: black onyx, black tourmaline, bloodstone (said to stop bleeding and treat diseases of the blood, such as feline leukemia), obsidian, red garnet, red jasper, ruby (believed by many healers to offer the greatest protection against bad health), and smoky quartz (protects a cat from unseen dangers).

Second: Sacral Chakra

Color ray: ORANGE-RED

Located halfway between the stomach and the pubic region, this chakra (also known as *svadhisthana*) relates to the following parts of a cat's body: genitals, kidneys, and the reproductive system. The gemstones that are traditionally used to heal this chakra are amber (which aids the birth of kittens), carnelian, and orange calcite.

Third: Solar Plexus Chakra

Color ray: YELLOW

Located in the middle of the abdomen, this chakra (also known as *manipurna*) relates to the following parts of a cat's body: the digestive system, liver, pancreas, small intestine, and stomach. The gemstones that are traditionally used to heal this chakra are: citrine (keeps a cat safe from harm), tiger's eye, yellow calcite, and yellow topaz.

Fourth: Heart Chakra

Color ray: GREEN

Located at the center of the chest, this chakra (also known as *anahata*) relates to the following parts of a cat's body: the chest, heart, lungs, front legs, and paws. It also influences immunity to disease. The gemstones that are traditionally used to heal this chakra are: aventurine, chrysoprase (calms and cures neurotic feline behavior), emerald, green tourmaline, malachite, pink tourmaline, peridot, rose quartz, and rhodochrosite (heals physical and emotional wounds in both man and beast).

Fifth: Throat Chakra

Color ray: BLUE

Located at the middle of the throat, this chakra (also known as *visuddha*) relates to the following parts of a cat's body: the

throat, neck, mouth, and shoulder blades. It also influences me-
tabolism. The gemstones that are traditionally used to heal this
chakra are: amazonite (said to induce a constant flow of health),
aquamarine, blue lace agate, blue topaz, chrysocolla, and tur-
quoise (a stone sacred to Native Americans).

Sixth: Brow or Third Eye Chakra

Color ray: INDIGO
Located at the forehead between the eyes, the chakra (also
known as *ajna*) relates to the following parts of a cat's body: the
brain, eyes, ears, and whiskers. The gemstones that are traditionally used to heal this chakra are: azurite, lapis lazuli (in addition to healing, this stone enhances a cat's psychic abilities),
sapphire, and sodalite.

Seventh: Crown Chakra

Color ray: VIOLET
Located at the top of the head, this chakra (also known as
sahasrara) relates to a cat's highest brain centers and spirit, as well
as to its entire physical body. It is said that the Crown Chakra
(the most spiritual of all the chakras) cannot be activated unless
the first six are put into balance. The gemstones that are traditionally used to heal this chakra are: amethyst (relieves pain and
nervousness), clear quartz, diamond, and fluorite.

Healing With Magickal Sachets

A witch's healing sachet for cats is not difficult to make, and
can be used to help a cat recover from an injury or illness. It
can also be used as a magickal charm to keep a healthy cat or
kitten safe from accidents and diseases.
To make one, place a square piece of white cloth (approximately three inches by three inches) on a tabletop or other flat
surface. In the center of the cloth, place a small cat's eye stone,

a pinch of vervain, a few caraway seeds, and three hairs from the cat's tail. Pull the four corners together and tie securely with a white ribbon or piece of string.

To consecrate and charge the sachet with power, place it upon an altar between two white cat-shaped candles. Light the candles, visualize a circle of fiery red light surrounding the altar, and say: *By the element of Fire, ancient and powerful, I consecrate and bless this sachet for use as a tool for healing (name of cat). Elemental spirits of Fire, I call upon thee now to empower this magickal tool with your blessings.*

Using a feather, trace the symbol of a pentagram in the air above the sachet. Visualize an ethereal cloud-white circle of light surrounding the altar, and say: *By the element of Air, ancient and powerful, I consecrate and bless this sachet for use as a tool for healing (name of cat). Elemental spirits of Air, I call upon thee now to empower this magickal tool with your blessings.*

Place a seashell upon the sachet. Visualize a circle of ocean-blue light surrounding the altar, and say: *By the element of Water, ancient and powerful, I consecrate and bless this sachet for use as a tool for healing (name of cat). Elemental spirits of Water, I call upon thee now to empower this magickal tool with your blessings.*

Remove the seashell from the sachet. Place a crystal, any magickal gemstone, or a healing rune over it. Visualize a dark, forest-green circle of light surrounding the altar, and say: *By the element of Earth, ancient and powerful, I consecrate and bless this sachet for use as a tool for healing (name of cat). Elemental spirits of Earth, I call upon thee now to empower this magickal tool with your blessings. So mote it be.*

Give thanks to the four elements for their magickal favors, and then extinguish the two cat-shaped candles on the altar using a candle snuffer or pinching out the flames with your moistened fingertips.

The ritual is now complete and the healing sachet is ready to be used. For best results, place it under the cat's bedding or attach it to the animal's collar, unless she takes a strong objection to it. If you desire, you may anoint the sachet once a week with three drops of the appropriate essential oil.

A Candlelight Spell for Healing

Using the tip of a consecrated ritual dagger, carve healing runes upon a white, cat-shaped candle. (If you wish, you may use a different tool, such as a dry pen or a nut pick, instead of a ritual dagger.) Also carve the symbol of your cat's astrological sign (if it is known), along with his name.

Anoint the candle with three drops of eucalyptus, lavender, lotus, myrrh, narcissus, or rosemary oil. (Each of these essential oils contain strong healing vibrations.) Light the candle, and then (if it is at all possible) hold the sick or injured cat in your arms as you recite the following prayer to the goddess Bastet:

O gracious lady Bastet, from your golden desert of dreams I call to thee. Come forth from the cat-filled temple where you dwell, feline goddess, woman of mystery. Bring thy healing powers and thy divine cat-magick. I ask that you take (name of cat) into thy loving arms and heal her, strengthen her, bless and protect her. O loving goddess Bastet, beautiful lady of Bubastis, I shower thee with praise and bid thee farewell for now. Return now to thy ancient land of the pharaohs, where the shadows of the Sphinx dance beneath the sacred light of Ra. Until our paths cross once more, blessed be!

The healing methods that have been outlined in this chapter are but a few examples of the many ways in which many modern witches, neo-pagans, and New Age folks use the powers of herbs, gemstones, and magickal spells to heal their feline friends and familiars.

Other popular methods of alternative healing for cats and other animals include, but are not limited to, aromatherapy, massage, Reiki, magnet therapy, the laying on of hands, and acupuncture.

Appendix: Resources

Abyss Distribution/AzureGreen
48 Chester Road
Chester, Massachusetts 01011
(413) 623-2155; Fax: (413) 623-2156

In addition to their impressive selection of metaphysical books, magickal herbs, New Age music, jewelry and ritual items, they offer both black cat and Egyptian cat-goddess candles, Bast pendants, cat amulets for protection from evil, and a wide selection of Tarot decks to choose from, including the popular *Tarot of the Cat People*.

American Holistic Veterinary Association
2214 Old Emmorton Road
Bel Air, Maryland 21014
(410) 569-0795

Angels Afoot
P.O. Box 3002
Joplin, Missouri 64803
(417) 781-7190

A catalogue of T-shirts, sweatshirts, tote bags, note cards and postcards for people who adore cat angels. Designs include winged cats, angelic cats, and cats sitting upon a crescent moon.

Cat Astrology by Michael Zullo
Order from: 3361 Flagler Avenue
Key West, Florida 33040
(305) 292-1068

Published in 1993, this 82-page hardcover book sells for $14.95 and is a "complete guide to feline horoscopes." If you love cats and astrology, then this delightful book is purr-fect for you!

Cat Faeries
260 Hazelwood Avenue
San Francisco, California 94127
(415) 585-6400

Catnip Flower Essence for cats. Also available: Meow Mist (a catnip floral water) and other flower essences.

Cat Goddess
2530 Berryessa Road (No. 935)
San Jose, California 95132

This company offers pendants, mugs, T-shirts, tote bags, and other items bearing the Egyptian cat-goddess (Bastet) design. Inquire for jewelry prices. They also make available a bronze cat-goddess statue for $20.00 plus $4.00 shipping and handling.

Catspells by Claire Nahmad
Order from: Running Press
125 South 22nd Street
Philadelphia, Pennsylvania 19103
(215) 568-2919

Published in 1993, over fifty Victorian-era magickal spells are included in this 88-page hardcover "collection of enchantments for you and your feline companion." Price: $12.95.

Catstars
Contact: Dr. Gary Miller
3033 East Thunderbird Road (No. 2023)
Phoenix, Arizona 85032
(602) 992-2193

This unique service will prepare an astrological chart, personality analysis, and planetary-based profile for your cat for only $19.95 plus $3.00 for shipping and handling. Write or call for more information.

Homeo Pet
   P.O. Box 147
   Westhampton Beach, New York 11978
   (800) 555-4461

Write or call for information about FDA-registered, 100 percent natural, homeopathic products that offer your cat a health-care alternative.

Purring in the Light: Near-Death Experiences of Cats by Stefanie Samek
   Order from: Plume Paperbacks
   375 Hudson Street
   New York, New York 10014
   (212) 366-2000

A 134-page collection of whimsical, mystical stories about cats' close
calls with death and otherworld phenomena. Published in 1995, this book
sells for $7.95.

The Whole Kitty CATalog by John Avalon Reed
   Crown Trade Paperbacks
   201 East 50th Street
   New York, New York 10022

Over 800 products designed with cats in mind, including toys, cat-care
products, books, gifts, gadgets, art, videos, and much more. Also contains
many True Cat Facts. Published in 1996, this 244-page book sells for
$19.95.

Zen for Cats: Teachings of the Zen Cat Masters by Alfred Birnbaum and
Riku Kanmei
   Order from: Weatherhill, Inc.
   420 Madison Avenue, 15th Floor
   New York, New York 10017
   (800) 437-7840

A humorous 90-page hardcover book that combines ancient Buddhist
philosophy with the inscrutability of cats. Published in 1993, this illustrated book sells for $9.95.

Bibliography

Ackroyd, Eric. *A Dictionary of Dream Symbols.* London: Blandford (an imprint of Cassell Villiers House), 1993.

Beadle, Muriel. *The Cat: History, Biology, and Behavior.* New York: Simon and Schuster, 1977.

Brasch, R. *Strange Customs: How Did They Begin?* New York: David McKay Company, Inc., 1976.

Bromage, B. *The Occult Arts of Ancient Egypt.* United Kingdom: Aquarian Press, 1953.

Bryant, Mark. *The Cat Name Companion.* Secaucus, N.J.: Citadel Press, 1995.

Burger, Carl. *All About Cats.* New York: Random House, 1966.

Caras, Roger A. *A Cat Is Watching.* New York: Simon and Schuster, 1989.

——— . *A Celebration of Cats.* New York: Simon and Schuster, 1986.

Carr, William H. A. *The Basic Book of the Cat.* New York: Charles Scribner's Sons, 1963.

Cavendish, Richard. *The Black Arts.* New York: Perigee Books, 1983.

Clutton-Brock, Juliet. *Cats: Ancient and Modern.* Cambridge, Mass.: Harvard University Press, 1993.

Conway, D. J. *The Mysterious, Magickal Cat.* St. Paul, Minn.: Llewellyn Publications, 1998.

Cunningham, Scott. *The Magickal Household.* St. Paul, Minn.: Llewellyn Publications, 1983.

Dale-Green, Patricia. *The Cult of the Cat.* London: William Heinemann Company, 1963.

Darnton, Robert. *The Great Cat Massacre.* New York: Basic Books, Inc., 1984.

DeLys, Claudia. *A Treasury of American Superstitions.* New York: Philosophical Library, 1948.

Dunwich, Gerina. *Wicca A to Z.* Secaucus, N.J.: Citadel Press, 1997.

————. *A Wiccan's Guide to Prophecy and Divination.* Secaucus, N.J.: Citadel Press, 1996.

Eckstein, Warren and Fay. *The Illustrated Cat's Life.* New York: Fawcett Columbine, 1990.

Fish, Enrica. *The Cat in Art.* Minneapolis, Minn.: Lerner Publications Company, 1970.

Fleischer, Leonore. *The Cat's Pajamas: A Charming and Clever Compendium of Feline Trivia.* New York: Harper and Row, 1982.

Frazier, Anitra and Norma Eckroate. *The New Natural Cat.* New York: Plume (an imprint of the New American Library, a division of Penguin Books U.S.A. Inc.:), 1990.

Gebhardt, Richard H.: consultant editor; Grace Pond and Dr. Ivor Raleigh: general editors. *A Standard Guide to Cat Breeds.* New York: McGraw-Hill Book Company, 1979.

Grilhe, Gillette. *The Cat and Man.* New York: Putnam, 1974.

Guiley, Rosemary Ellen. *The Encyclopedia of Witches and Witchcraft.* New York: Facts on File, 1989.

Hean-Tatt, Ong. *Chinese Animal Symbols.* Malaysia: Pelanduk Publications, 1993.

Henderson, G. N. and D. J. Coffey, editors. *The International Encyclopedia of Cats.* New York: McGraw-Hill Book Co., 1973.

Howey, M. Oldfield. *The Cat in the Mysteries of Religion and Magic.* New York: Castle Books, 1956.

Jay, Roni. *Mystic Cats.* United Kingdom: Godsfield Press, 1995.

Jordan, Michael. *Encyclopedia of Gods.* New York: Facts on File, 1993.

Lorie, Peter. *Superstitions.* New York: Simon and Schuster, 1992.

Mackenzie, Donald A. *Egyptian Myth and Legend.* New York: Bell Publishing Company, 1978.

Mayo, Jeff and Christine Ramsdale. *Astrology.* Lincolnwood, Ill.: NTC Publishing Group, 1996.

McCoy, Edain. *A Witch's Guide to Faery Folk.* St. Paul, Minn.: Llewellyn Publications, 1994.

Mery, Fernand. *The Life, History, and Magic of the Cat.* New York: Grosset and Dunlap, 1966.

Morris, Desmond. *Catlore.* New York: Crown Publishers, 1987.

————. *Catwatching.* New York: Crown Publishers, 1986.

Patrick, Richard. *All Color Book of Egyptian Mythology.* Secancus, N.J.: Chartwell Books, Inc., 1989.

Poe, Edgar Allan. *Complete Stories and Poems of Edgar Allan Poe.* Garden City, N.Y.: Doubleday and Company, Inc., 1966.

Pond, Grace, editor. *The Complete Cat Encyclopedia*. New York: Crown Publishers, 1972.

Reader's Digest Illustrated Book of Cats. Montreal: The Reader's Digest Association (Canada) Ltd., 1992.

Reed, John Avalon. *The Whole Kitty CATalog*. New York: Crown Trade Paperbacks, 1996.

Rice, Edward and Jean Gleason. *Cats, Cats, and Cats*. New York: Creative Age Press, Inc., 1947.

Robbins, Rossell Hope. *The Encyclopedia of Witchcraft and Demonology*. New York: Bonanza Books, 1981.

Sawyer, Angela. *Cats: A Guide to Breeding and Showing*. New York: Arco Publishing, Inc., 1983.

Seymour-Smith, Martin. *The New Astrology*. New York: Collier Books/MacMillan Publishing Company, 1981.

Shaw, Eva. *Divining the Future*. New York: Facts on File, 1995.

Siegal, Mordecai, editor. *Simon and Schuster's Guide to Cats*. New York: Simon and Schuster, 1983.

Sillar, F. C. and R. M. Meyler. *Cats: Ancient and Modern*. New York: The Viking Press, 1966.

South, M., editor. *Topsell's Histories of Beasts*. Chicago: Nelson-Hall, 1981.

Spies, Joseph R. *The Compleat Cat*. Englewood Cliffs, N.J.: Prentice-Hall, Inc., 1984.

Sproule, Anna and Michael. *The Complete Cat*. New York: Multimedia Books Limited, 1994.

Steeh, Judith. *Cats*. Greenwich, Conn.: Bison Books, 1983.

Steiger, Brad. *Totems: The Transformative Power of Your Personal Animal Totem*. New York: Harper Collins, 1997.

Suares, Jean-Claude. *Great Cats: The Who's Who of Famous Felines*. New York: Bantam Books, 1981.

———. *The Indispensible Cat*. New York: Stewart Tabori and Chang, 1983.

Unkelbach, Kurt. *Catnip: Selecting and Training Your Cat*. Englewood Cliffs, N.J.: Prentice-Hall, Inc., 1970.

Walker, Barbara G. *The Woman's Encyclopedia of Myths and Secrets*. San Francisco: Harper and Row, 1983.

Waring, Philippa. *A Dictionary of Omens and Superstitions*. New York: Ballantine Books, 1978.

White, Suzanne. *Suzanne White's Book of Chinese Chance*. New York: M. Evans and Company, 1976.

———— . *Suzanne White's Guide to Love*. San Francisco: Harper San Francisco, 1996.

Whitfield, Susan and Philippa-Alys Browne. *The Animals of the Chinese Zodiac*. New York: Crocodile Books USA, 1998.

Wright, Michael and Sally Walters, editors. *The Book of the Cat*. New York: Summit Books, 1980.

Zeuner, F. E. *A History of Domesticated Animals*. London: Hutchinson, 1963.

Index

About the Author

GERINA DUNWICH (whose first name is pronounced with a soft G) is a High Priestess of the Old Religion and an ordained minister (Universal Life Church). Born under the sign of Capricorn, Gerina is also a professional astrologer and Tarot reader, the editor and publisher of *Golden Isis* (a pagan literary journal), the founder of both the Pagan Poets Society and the Wheel of Wisdom School, a poet, and a cat-lover. She considers herself to be a life-long student of the occult and is the author of numerous books on the spell-casting arts and the earth-oriented religion of Wicca. She writes and plays music and has lived in various parts of the world, including a 300-year-old Colonial house near Salem, Massachusetts, and a haunted Victorian mansion in upstate New York.

She currently lives in Chatsworth, California, with her Gemini soul mate and a golden-eyed, ginger tabby cat–familiar named Gemini. Reach her by E-mail at witchywoman13@usa.net.